BASED ON A
TRUE STORY

BASED ON A
TRUE
STORY

[A MEMOIR]

NORM
MACDONALD

SPIEGEL & GRAU / NEW YORK

Copyright © 2016 by Norm Macdonald
Foreword copyright © 2016 by Louis C.K.

All rights reserved.

Published in the United States by Spiegel & Grau, an imprint of Random House, a division of
Penguin Random House LLC, New York.

SPIEGEL & GRAU and Design is a registered trademark of Penguin Random House LLC.

Grateful acknowledgment is made to Sony/ATV Music Publishing LLC for
permission to reprint an excerpt from "Willy the Wandering Gypsy and Me"
by Billy Joe Shaver, copyright © 1972 by Sony/ATV Music Publishing LLC.
All rights administered by Sony/ATV Music Publishing LLC, 424 Church Street,
Suite 1200, Nashville, TN 37219. All rights reserved. Used by permission.

All photographs are reproduced courtesy of the author.

Library of Congress Cataloging-in-Publication Data
Names: Macdonald, Norm.
Title: Based on a true story / by Norm Macdonald.
Description: First edition. | New York : Spiegel & Grau, 2016.
Identifiers: LCCN 2016014108| ISBN 9780812993622 (hardback) |
ISBN 9780812993639 (ebook)
Subjects: LCSH: Macdonald, Norm. | Comedians—Canada—Biography. | Actors—
Canada—Biography. | BISAC: BIOGRAPHY & AUTOBIOGRAPHY / Entertainment &
Performing Arts. | BIOGRAPHY & AUTOBIOGRAPHY / Personal Memoirs.
Classification: LCC PN2308.M23 A3 2016 | DDC 792.7/6028092 [B]—dc23
LC record available at https://lccn.loc.gov/2016014108

Printed in the United States of America on acid-free paper

randomhousebooks.com

spiegelandgrau.com

4 6 8 9 7 5 3

Book design by Susan Turner

To Charles Manson (not that one)

Three fingers whiskey pleasures the drinkers,
Moving does more than that drinking for me.
Willy, he tells me that doers and thinkers
Say moving's the closest thing to being free.
—BILLY JOE SHAVER,
"Willy the Wandering Gypsy and Me"

To live outside the law you must be honest.
—BOB DYLAN,
"Absolutely Sweet Marie"

I know of only two very real evils in life: remorse and illness.
—LEO TOLSTOY,
War and Peace

LOUIS C.K.

first saw Norm Macdonald onstage in 1988. I was twenty-one years old and he came to headline a club in Boston where I had been doing stand-up for three years. Me and my friends had heard about him, so I went to check him out.

Within two minutes I was astonished by how goddamn funny he was. Just blown away. I laughed harder that night than I had in my life. I remember my comedian friends and I just sat and talked about him for hours after the show. I went back to see him five times during the week he was at that club. He instantly became my favorite comedian, and in the thirty years since, he has never stumbled far from that rank. Every time I see or hear Norm, he's doing something new and better than the last time—he gives me a new favorite comedy bit.

The thing that drives me nuts about Norm is the powerful simplicity of his style. A lot of comics (myself included) swagger around the stage and fly into contrived bits of anger that give them an air of dynamic importance. Norm has a beguiling humility that sneaks up and grabs you by the throat. There is something about how simply Norm says things onstage. Just lays words end to end with such elegance. And then you just explode with laughter and you just can't stop. He's just standing there talking and you're howling and trying to breathe, your head in your lap. The power in that is amazing.

Norm is brilliant and thoughtful, and there is sensitivity and creative insight in his observations and stories. But really he's just talking. Just a guy talking and somehow shredding everything he talks about.

He mildly dives into dark and light subjects alike and fabricates them with his hand in his pocket and his wry look. And he leaves you limp. How does he do it? I don't know. I have been a student of comedy my whole life and I honestly don't know how he does any of it. He has a fastball and a slider and about fifty arm angles.

A lot of comics over the years have been compared to Mark Twain, but I think Norm is the only one who actually matches the guy in terms of his voice and ability.

I listened to Norm on the radio once with my fourteen-year-old daughter, and he was doing a bit about how he would go about stalking, abducting, murdering, and burying a woman. Just politely explaining what would be his logistical plan. My daughter and I were dying laughing. Just cackling and howling. How do you get a forty-eight-year-old man and a fourteen-year-old girl to laugh like *that* together? And he could have told that same bit to a bunch of ladies at a church and they would have laughed just as hard.

I really could go on and on about Norm. He's a brilliant comedian. One of the greatest of all time. I put him in my top five.

The last thing is that there is not one single other comedian like him. He falls into no genre or category. Just comedian.

I seriously fucking love Norm Macdonald. Please buy his book. He probably needs the cash. He's really bad with money.

FOUND ALIVE IN A HOTEL ROOM
IN EDMONTON

"You're dead."

"The hell I am!" They'll see.

I've heard this kind of talk before. How I'm finished, through, obsolete, passé, yesterday's news, a has-been, a fossil.

"I'll have you know I'm just as relevant today as I was twenty-five years ago."

"No, no," my agent laughs through the phone, like it's the greatest joke in the world. "Check your Wikipedia page. You're dead all right."

I look around the room and see the small bottles that are scattered everywhere, those small bottles that make me feel so big. They're empty now, of course, just like me. My suitcase is in the corner—same one I've had my whole career—and it's all beat to hell, stitching coming outta the sides, but it still does its job. Sorta.

Stand-up comedy is a shabby business, made up of shabby fellows like me who cross the country, stay at shabby hotels, and tell jokes they no longer find funny. You show up in a strange town, and next thing, you're gone. Then another town, and another, and another. Then a thousand more. Then another. You're moving, always moving, like a criminal drifter, getting what you can from a place and then getting out. You're never in one place long enough to experience anything but the shabbiest of love.

I turn to look at the girl next to me in bed. I must have met her last night at the comedy club, where they had a great tall picture of me leaning against the door to remind the people what a bigshot I once was. Her hair is bright yellow, her lips are bright red, and she'll wake up soon and I'll pretend that I remember her. I make my way quietly through the dim room to the wide-open minibar. It's empty but for one tiny bottle way at the back. I always leave one. I drink her dry, the way a man puts gas in his car when the tank's near empty. Just to keep going a little longer down the endless road.

Damn near fifty.

Over at the table I hit a couple of buttons on my computer and discover what my agent found so funny. Some joker has changed my Wikipedia page, all right, and he's left me for dead. "Norm Macdonald (October 17, 1963–May 12, 2013) *was* a comedian and actor who *was* known from . . ." I read on and on till the final sentence. The death sentence. "Mr. Macdonald was found dead in an Edmonton hotel room from an overdose of morphine."

Well, that's a sight to see, all right, with all the authority of the Internet behind it! I'm standing stock-still in the very same Edmonton hotel room where I'd died the night before. And then I start to laugh and I laugh to beat all get-out, just like my agent did, just because I'm alive and I can. Then a thought comes to me in a sudden, a thought that stops all my laughing, makes me real cold, and has me craving a couple of grains of morphine, or at least some whiskey. And the thought is this: *The preposterous lie on the screen before me isn't that far off.* After all, the only thing this joker really did was change tenses, turned "does" to "did" and "is" to "was." He got the date of my passing wrong, for sure, but nothing else. To misquote

Twain, it turns out the rumor of my death is only slightly exaggerated.

So now I start to read this thing on the computer again, only this time I read it the way I imagine a stranger will in a few years or a few decades. When it's true. In the future, when I *was* Norm Macdonald. So this is my life, then, these words on this screen? Well, it doesn't add up to much, just a series of facts, and I suppose that's what a man's life is, after all, but it's more than that too. I mean, it has to be, doesn't it? And so I decide I will write an account of my life my own self. My side of the story.

Damn near fifty.

The girl on the bed is beginning to stir now and I feel sorry for her, the same way I feel sorry for myself every time I have to wake up. I struggle to remember her name, but it's no good. And as I look at her and wonder who we were last night, I come up with a title for my book. I'll call it *Based on a True Story,* because it comes to me that there's no way of telling a true story. I mean a really true one, because of memory. It's just no good.

It's like when a guy is telling a story and he's way off and you know he is because the whole story is about you. But he's changing it all around, leaving out important parts and making up others from whole cloth, doing whatever he has to do to turn the dead stuff of life into something worth telling. And you'd correct him, but the thing is, you're not sure you remember it a hundred percent accurately yourself. It turns out your memory isn't the precise court stenographer you think it is, getting every word down just so. It's more like the sketch artist way at the back of the courtroom who is doing his level best to capture images that no longer are.

So it won't be a true story. It'll be based on a true story, like every story I've ever told. But I promise you this: It'll be the truth, every word of it, to the best of my memory. And I won't just scratch the surface either, no sirree, Bob. I'll claw and tear into this showbiz career of mine and I'll let the filth fly, like a mad dog digging up bones he buried deep and long ago. And I'll name names. And I'll drop bombshells. I bet they'll pay good money for that kinda thing. For the straight dope on the Hollywood crowd, and the *SNL*ers too. And I need money. I need money to live.

Damn near fifty.

I open the curtains and it's raining outside. I catch an image of myself in the window, and the rain blurs my thin reflection as if I'm barely there at all. And I see there's a bruise under my left eye and some dried blood. I look down at my hand, and the heel of my thumb is swollen purple and hurts like a bastard and that makes me happy. It means the girl on the bed was fought for and not bought.

She's full awake now, and she's holding her head and squinting and I watch her as she sees me. I can tell she doesn't remember anything either. Well, that's okay. I'll hear all about it later from the guy who runs the comedy club and I'll sit and listen, transfixed, to the forgotten details of last night and shake my head, bewildered, feeling like a trespasser in my own life.

I look at the girl squarely. "I'll get us a bottle."

She has a pretty smile.

BASED ON A
TRUE STORY

THE JOB INTERVIEW

"Lorne will see you now."

He was always Lorne, never Mr. Michaels. He was smart that way. I took a seat across the desk from him, and there was a container of pencils that had been sharpened that very day and a bowl of fresh popcorn and plenty of Coca-Cola.

"Swell office you got here, Lorne."

"Thank you, Norm. I understand you're from Canada?"

"Yes, sir," I said, and I knew that even though we hailed from the same nation, we were worlds apart. He was a cosmopolite from Toronto, worldly, the kinda guy who'd be comfortable around the Queen of England herself. Me, I was a hick, born to the barren, rocky soil of the Ottawa Valley, where the richest man in town was the barber. Lorne was a bigshot and I was a smallfry, and that's why I was planning on doing very little talking in this job interview.

First let me say that Lorne is often portrayed as an intimidating man, and he is. In some ways he can't help it. He is quietly confident, smart, funny, and he always carries a dagger. These four qualities combine to make for an intimidating man.

He had beautiful assistants that the writers had derisively nick-named "the Lornettes." These girls secretly loved Lorne and also openly loved him. In another room, the writers sat around and did impressions of Lorne that didn't sound anything like him. This is the way it is with all bigshots and all smallfrys everywhere, and it's been like that since the get-go. The boss is always a big joke, just dumb and lucky, and nobody's afraid of him at all and everybody has a good laugh at him. Until he walks into the room, that is. It's a different story then.

Lorne began the interview by telling stories, and I just listened and nodded and laughed when I was supposed to, the same way I did in every job interview I'd ever had. But this guy was different. First thing I noticed was that he was funny, really genuinely funny, and that is very rare for a bigshot. Especially a bigshot in comedy.

He had all these firsthand stories he was telling me about back in the day when he worked on shows in Toronto and then in Hollywood. And he smiled when he told the stories, the kind of smile a man gets when memory transports him to another place and another time. He had worked on *The Smothers Brothers Comedy Hour* and a few Lily Tomlin specials. And there were famous celebrities in his stories, and all the stories were funny. And pretty soon my pretend laugh was turning into an honest-to-God real laugh, and I was choking on popcorn and coughing Coca-Cola.

We were having a grand old time until suddenly Lorne got down to business. "So, Norm, let me tell you how the audition process works. We go down to the studio and you show us two characters."

I hadn't expected this. I'd been told this meeting was a mere formality, that as long as I didn't insult Lorne outright, the job was mine.

I'd been misinformed.

"Well, you see, Lorne, the thing is this. I'm a nightclub comic. Jokes, crowd work, that kinda thing. But I'm a hard worker and I catch on really fast. Besides, I understand I've been vouched for." And I had been too. By Jim Downey, the head writer and second-in-command. By David Spade, the comic actor. Why, even by Adam Sandler himself!

"Yes, I've heard good things. But the thing is, you're a stand-up comedian. We are a variety show and I have to be sure you will be able to provide versatility. I don't want to waste your time or mine." I wasn't sure he cared about wasting my time, since I'd been left in his waiting room for four hours, waiting and waiting. And waiting.

"Tell me another story about Lily Tomlin, Lorne," I blurted out. I figured if he could tell me another funny story, I could start laughing again, and we could go back to those great times we were having a few moments ago. But no dice.

Then he unsmiled his lips and got real plural on me. "We'll let you know," he said, and he looked down at a blank piece of paper on his desk. Well, you'd think he was a generous hatter and I was the tallest man in the whole wide world, the way he gave me the high hat that day.

I staggered to my feet, sweating hard, and chugged down the last of the Coca-Cola as Lorne meticulously studied that blank piece of paper the way I'd imagine a sculptor might study a mountain of rock. I had to think and think fast. But that's not easy for me. I think slow. Real slow.

I felt like I was back in first grade and I'd just failed, as I always did. But that made me think of something else. You see, a lot of times, when I hadn't finished my homework, I would bring the teacher a shiny red apple and present it to her. It would always work, of course. What would a teacher rather do, read scribbled nonsense from a five-year-old or eat a shiny red apple?

But I wasn't dealing with a first-grade teacher here. This was the legendary Lorne Michaels, and he wasn't known for changing his mind once it was made up. Was there a chance I could redapple the old man? I didn't know. But I did know I was lucky enough that day to have a shiny red apple in my back pocket.

Well, I didn't have an actual shiny red apple. That would have been perfect. But that's not how things work in this here life. I did happen to have the closest thing to a shiny red apple in my back pocket. My actual back pocket.

"Listen, Lorne, I do have one character I've been working on, and I think it'll be a big hit. The biggest. But I don't want to do it down in the studio, where some bum might steal it and take it for his own. I want to do it just for you, right here and now."

Lorne looked up at me with that stare of his that passeth all human understanding. "Go ahead, Norm."

I reached inside my back pocket and pulled out a bag containing seven grams of government-grade morphine and two brand-new syrettes and tossed them on his desk.

"I call this character 'The Connection.' "

"Norm, I confess that your antics are near amusing, but this is not what we at the show refer to as a 'character.' Do you know what we call this at the show, Norm?"

"No, sir. What?"

"A recurring character."

I was in.

2

A DEBT UNPAID

've been on the road a pickler's fortnight and I'm dog-tired.

A great deal of time has passed since the girl with the bright-yellow hair and the bright-red lips told me that my writing a book wasn't the worst idea she'd ever heard. Since then, I traveled all the way to New York City to meet with a publisher. The publisher is a girl, and it's about time, I say. Her name is Julie and she has brown hair and red lips. She got me a secretary who's good at typing and I've been working nonstop. I spent a month in New York to begin writing the book. I'm two paragraphs into my second chapter and I'm looking forward to being a bigshot author. And why not? New York City was the site of my great success. I made it there and then I didn't make it anywhere else. I guess Frank Sinatra isn't so smart after all.

I'm finally home in Los Angeles and I'm at the very back table of The World Famous Comedy Store. I sit alone, surrounded by black. That's what I like about this place. The walls are black and the floors are black and the tables are black, and that suits me just fine. Everybody looks pretty much the same in the black. On my table sits a bottle of Wild Turkey 101 and there is a glass beside it. The glass is bone-dry—just there for appearance. The bottle is half full. There's a guy up onstage and I think he's saying some pretty important things, because people are clapping a lot and shaking their heads sadly.

"Why don't you do a set?" says Adam Eget.

"Nobody wants to see me do a set."

"Sure they do. They love you! They'll get a big kick out of it."

Adam Eget is the manager of The World Famous Comedy Store. As always, he has a lit cigarette stuck to his bottom lip, he shifts his eyes from side to side, and he looks like he wants to be anywhere other than here, all of which conspire to give him the look of a getaway-car driver. And he doesn't know it yet, but soon he'll be just that.

Adam Eget always wears a suit, the kind of suit a poor man thinks a rich man wears. He's a man who acts like a bigshot but he knows I know what he is. He was a smallfry when I met him and he's a smallfry now. I've known him for a right smart spell, since my days at SNL in New York City, New York. That's where I found him, making a living underneath the Queensboro Bridge, jerking off punks for fifteen dollars a man. He said he was eighteen at the time, and he looked considerably younger, but he had a car so I made him my assistant. I figured I'd let him work at 30 Rockefeller Center, where his job was to do whatever it was I said—to make all my wishes real. He was good at it. Some men are just born to do other men's bidding, and Adam Eget is such a man. It's a gift that pocketed him plenty in the shadow of the bridge. And he can wear his big man's suit and order around waitresses and busboys all he wants, but it doesn't impress me one bit. Like I said before, I know what he is and he knows that I know it.

"Why don't you sit down and have a drink with me?" I say.

"Norm, I've been sober for five years, three months, and twelve days. You know that."

"Well, then it sounds like you're due," I tell him. And then, to punctuate my fine joke, I take a comically oversize swig from my bottle.

The plain truth is that Adam Eget is an alcoholic and that's why he doesn't drink. Me, I'm not an alcoholic and that's why I do drink. Life sure is funny that way.

But my heart goes out to Adam Eget because an addiction is a deep hook, and sometimes the harder you wriggle to escape her, the deeper she goes. I should know, because I've got one of my own. I like to gamble—gamble money on games of chance. And some have said that it's been the ruin of me.

"Go up and do a set. They'll love you. They're a great crowd."

"So you're saying they're such a great crowd that they'll even love the likes of me?"

"No, you know that's not what I'm saying. C'mon, Norm, as a favor to me. I promise they'll get a big kick out of it."

There's a lady up onstage now and she's saying the most unladylike things, quite shocking. The folks in the crowd are looking at each other, astonished. They can hardly believe what they're hearing and I can tell that they don't know what to do, so they decide to laugh.

"Fine," I say. "I'll do a set."

I shamble onto the stage. In stand-up, what you wear is very important. Some comics wear a pair of jeans and a T-shirt, trying to look like a regular Joe so the crowd will relate to them. Others take the stage sporting a ten-thousand-dollar suit, as a sign of respect for the folks who came to hear them. Me, I wear just the same thing I wear offstage: a *Norm Show* T-shirt, an *SNL* jacket, and a *Dirty Work* hat. I figure, in show business, it never hurts to remind the folks just exactly who you are.

I open with my surefire bit about answering machines, and the crowd doesn't get a big kick out of it at all. I continue to talk and the words come out the same way they have for thirty years, but those words are only on my lips. In my mind a plan is hatching.

The plan has just somehow appeared in the emptiness of my brain, and in the black silence of the black room, this plan is bright as a sun. I don't dare leave the cold, bare stage until the entire plan unspools. And when it finally fully reveals itself to me in all its God-made glory, I thank the silent crowd and take my leave.

I stumble offstage to sarcastic applause, and some guy throws out his leg. I trip over it and go sprawling until my head hits something that's harder than my head, and this whole scene gets a bigger laugh than any of my jokes onstage did. I stagger to my feet and think about slugging the sonofabitch one. There was a time when I would have too, but that was when I was young. Now the world is young and I'm a weak old man.

I spot Adam Eget in the shadows.

"Sorry, Norm, I thought it was a good crowd. Guess I misread them."

"Gotta be able to read to misread," I say, and laugh loudly at my own quick wit.

"Touché," says Adam Eget.

I hate when people say "touché" after you say something funny. I don't know what it means, but I know that I hate it.

"Anyway, it was my fault. I shouldn't have convinced you to go up there."

"Best thing you could have done, Adam Eget."

"But they didn't laugh at a single thing you said!"

"It's not about what I spoke but what was spoke to me," I say, and Adam Eget looks puzzled. I know I'm not making a lick of sense, but I'm happy and frightened at the same time, and I generally don't like feeling two things at once unless they are very similar things.

"A plan came to me. Get the Challenger and bring her around. We're going to Vegas tonight!"

"I can't, Norm. I'm the manager here now. I'm an important man with responsibilities. I can't just leave work."

"They'll have to find another chimp," I say. "Get the car!"

"Norm, I'm not your assistant anymore. I'm my own man."

"You don't remember what happened on the boardwalk of Atlantic City, Adam Eget? It's been some time but I thought you might remember."

"I remember." And that is that. Adam Eget just shakes his head and looks real sick. He's certainly about to lose his job and everything he's worked to achieve. The simple fact is, Adam Eget has a debt unpaid. It's two decades old but I'm calling in my markers, so what choice does he have? He just nods his head a little and makes his way to the parking lot as I finish the bottle of Wild Turkey 101 and smile at the simple perfection of the plan. The plan that came from God Himself and revealed itself to me in the unlikeliest of places. Adam Eget pulls the car around and I get in. He drops me off at Sullivan's Boarding House. I pack all my *Norm Show* T-shirts, *Dirty Work* hats, and *SNL* jackets while he waits in the car. Then we are gone, moving fast, tearing the tar off Highway 15 all the way to Las Vegas, Nevada, aiming the white Challenger directly into the blood-red moon like a snowball rolling straight to hell.

3

MY FIRST FIVE YEARS

t doesn't take me long to understand I should have waited a little before this drive to Vegas. Adam Eget worked all night. Setting off in the smallest morning hours for a five-hour drive with a clown at the wheel who refuses to take the magic pills that keep you awake is just plain stupid. But there's something about Las Vegas that makes you want to be there right now. The white Challenger is having trouble staying in its lane and Adam Eget has a heavy-lidded look to him. In front of us a semi full of trembling logs weaves close, and as its tail takes a swipe at the Challenger I yell and Adam Eget gives his head a quick shake.

I know I'd better tell him a story, give him something to focus on. That's the job of a passenger in a car on a long road trip, after all. So I pull out a vial of liquid morphine and sink my cigarette in it. The narcotic dries fast, adhering to the tobacco. I light up and inhale deeply, listening to the wondrous crackling as the fire hits my lungs and the smoke hits my brain. Then the smoke clears and in the place where it was is now a picture.

The picture is of a tough old farm, a hundred acres of Godforsaken hard and unyielding soil, with a broke-down house and a barn that's in even worse shape—red paint is peeling down its sides like dried blood. There are thirty head of dairy cattle, fifty chickens, five hungry hogs, and one obsolete mule. And there are seven hicks there as well.

There, in the field, I see my father, scythe in hand, sweating hard as the hay falls before him. He works from sun to moon, stopping only for moments to wipe his already soaked handkerchief across his ruddy brow.

At the well, my mother is pumping water from a hundred feet below the earth and filling buckets that should be too heavy for such a slight young woman. On the porch of my home, my grandmother is sitting in a hardwood chair with an ax in her hand, and dancing in broken circles with a roaring fountain of blood where its head should be is a Dominicker hen. Tonight's dinner.

I turn my head toward the car window but I see no desert. I see the north forty, where Old Jack, the hired hand and the best man I've ever known, is driving a tractor twice as old as he is. The tractor has an orange triangle on its back and it bounces over the uneven earth. It's plain to see that the small hard seat is hurting Old Jack. In the wagon behind the tractor is my younger brother, Leslie, squealing delight in a carnival of hay bales.

Walking down the lane, with long arms full of short logs, is my older brother, Neil. Neil is the only one of us kids who has to do chores. He is nine years old. My grandmother says he's between grass and hay.

I see the cat, who's licking himself and swatting horseflies with his tail as he lies beneath an improbably large maple tree that is blighted and dying. I look up the tree and see there is something up high too, hiding in one of the crooks of its reaching branches. Something that is watching.

And the back of my head hits the headrest as I see that the thing in the tree is me.

I look to Adam Eget and see that he is beginning to drift away, and I understand that I have been silent this whole time. I take a long drag from my magic cigarette, close my eyes again, and a new and brighter picture displays itself before me. I begin to speak what it is that I see.

When I was young I was in great shape. I was in my peak physical condition back when I was one. Man, I looked great. I even looked good for my age. Strangers would always approach me, smiling, and they'd say, "Look at you, little boy, what are you, zero?"

"Oh, no," my mother would giggle. "He's one."

"Well, I'll be danged. He doesn't look a day past zero."

"No, he's one." She'd blush proudly. My mother did all my talking for me back then because I hadn't gotten the hang of it yet.

Back then my best friend was the cat, who only knew one word, "meow," but at the time it was one more word than I knew. I thought the cat had it all figured out. While my mother and father raced and chased through the world, the cat luxuriated on the hard wooden floor. His eyes were green and shone like the moon. And when the cat rubbed up against my belly, I could feel his purr deep inside me, as if I was the one purring, and this made me feel just as happy as a cat.

Those were sweet days, I'm here to tell you. Mostly on account of the way everyone was so mightily impressed by anything I'd do. And I mean anything! I'd walk into the room, holding a grape.

"Look who has a grape! Aren't you the smartest boy in the whole wide world?"

Sometimes all I had to do was show up.

"Look who it is! Did you come out to see what was going on in here? Aren't you the smartest boy in the whole wide world?"

Truth is, everyone had to be somewhere and I was there, that's all, just as they all were, but I wasn't gonna turn down any of those compliments. They thought I was pretty special, all right, and that was fine by me. It seemed like life was gonna be nothing but swell, with me spending my time doing what I damned pleased and everybody else spending their time being impressed.

All that changed one day when I was about three years old. I came busting into the parlor, where my folks were sitting with my grandma, and in my hand was a grape.

"Look here," I said, just as proud as sin. "I found another grape."

"Then eat the damn thing," said my father.

"You'll do no such thing!" my mother told me, and then turned to my father. "There's no telling where he found it."

I was frightened and confused, because I sensed something had changed irrevocably. As I left the room I heard my grandma say, "Is there something wrong with that boy?"

I loved my grandmother. Everything she did had to do with the making of food for the rest of us. I would lie on the cold linoleum of the kitchen floor and watch her work. My favorite was when she'd reduce vinegar. When vinegar is reduced, it becomes its own essence; all that is not neces-

sary evaporates. And my grandmother said that all it takes for that reduction to take place is time. Just time.

There was a picture of my grandmother on the kitchen wall, a picture of her as a young woman, and I would look between the picture and my grandmother and be unable to recognize each in the other. In the picture she was plump and large. Outside the picture she was thin and shrunken; there was no fat on her at all. I could see the way her flesh draped over her bones and sometimes I would shudder.

And of course there was Old Jack, who to this day is the most unforgettable fellow I've ever met. My father once told me how he had come to be hired. Seems Old Jack just showed up one day and asked if there was work to be had.

"Plenty of work," my father replied, "but can't afford you."

"Then I'll work for nothing," said Old Jack.

And so he did. Old Jack lived in a toolshed way back in the north forty, and for his work he got three squares a day and that was it. But I think he got more than that—because Old Jack never mentioned family or home, and so I think he got that in the deal too.

My favorite times were in the evening when my father would have company over. That's what we called it back then—company—and the old men would show up at the house and take a chair and a beer and they'd cracker-barrel the night away. My father was old when I was born. He was two generations before me. Years before he met my young mother, he had served in the war. All our neighbors were my father's age, so I was always around old ones growing up, and that suited me just fine. There was Bill Delaney, who could fix anything needed fixing. And Tommy Jackson, the town barber. One time he had a hippie from Cornwall come in for a trim but Tommy forced a proper haircut on him. There was Angus Macgregor, and he was a fine fellow for the most part, but when he hit the jug too deep his words would start to get obscene, and then profane, and then my father would lay a cross look on him and Angus would lower his eyes and make his words clean. And, of course, there was always Old Jack.

They'd tell stories from the old days, from the war and from the

Depression, and they'd tell jokes too. My father would always tell the best jokes, and after the punchline, everybody would laugh to beat the band, including my father. And then, as the laughter was dying down, my father would repeat the punchline and everybody would start laughing again.

The best joke I remember my father telling was the one about the old fellow whose memory was failing him.

"Did you ever hear tell of the old fellow who's having trouble remembering things so he goes to the doctor and the doctor prescribes him a medicine?"

"Don't believe I have, Lloyd," said Angus.

"Well, his friend comes over one day and says 'Jim, I understand you got some medicine for your memory. Tell me, does it work?'

" 'Oh, yes,' says Jim. 'Works like a charm.'

" 'Well, I'd like to get some of that medicine for myself. What's the name of it?'

" 'Oh, the name of it . . . ' says Jim. 'I can't remember. What's the name of that flower?'

" 'Oh, I don't know,' says Jim's friend. 'There's so many. Is it a tulip?'

" 'No. It's that flower you take on a date with a woman.'

" 'Oh, is it a carnation?'

" 'No, no. It's the romantic one. It's red, and long-stemmed.'

" 'Oh, you must mean a rose!'

" 'Yes that's it,' says Jim. 'ROSE, WHAT WAS THE NAME OF THAT MEDICINE THE DOCTOR GAVE ME FOR MY MEMORY?' "

Everybody would laugh hard and my father the hardest of all, and then, just as the laughter began to subside, he'd repeat, "ROSE, WHAT WAS THE NAME OF THAT MEDICINE?" and everybody would laugh harder still.

I would laugh too, sitting cross-legged in the corner. I loved all my dad's jokes.

But the real stories were better than the jokes, of course. They were tales of when these old men were young men, living through the

Depression, when there was nothing to be had, and if you couldn't find work there was no government to bail you out so you just went hungry. My dad became a railroad bum during those times. He owned nothing in the whole world but his own soul and even that, he knew, could be taken from him. He kept busy avoiding people like Kitchener Leslie, an infamous Canadian National Railway cop who was much scarier than the real police. If he found a bum on the property of CN Railway—sitting in an empty boxcar of a train—he would stomp and stomp with his steel-toed boots till the railroad bum was gone and only the gray, still flesh of the bum remained in his place.

Of course, the men told stories of when war came to Europe and turned scared boys from Moose Creek into heroes at Normandy. Old Jack, he could tell the best stories, because his were the most mysterious. It seemed Old Jack never had a home, that he somehow just sprang from the land itself, full grown, and had been roving his whole life till he settled down with us. He'd been in the war too, just like the rest of them, but he never told a single war story. His tales were about wandering the Cana-dian byways, filled with drink and song and loneliness and new places and friends, and they always held the other old men in thrall. And me too. I had never made it past Moose Creek and I knew I never would.

Round about ten o'clock the men would be on their way, taking the happy loudness with them and leaving the farmhouse quieter than the crickets and the frogs outside. Then Old Jack would say "Thank you" to my dad and "See you, Sprite" to me before he trundled out and down the lane to the tool-shed that was his home.

4

SIX YEARS OLD TO EIGHT YEARS OLD

One day when I was six years old, I came to know a truth, a hard truth that would stay with me for the rest of my life. I was in the farmhouse alone and I happened to look out the screen door, where I saw our cat. She was crouching close to the ground and utterly still, except for her tail, which switched like a metronome, side to side. I could see the cat's muscles roiling beneath her blue-gray fur. Her eyes shone fire upon a mouse that sat roughly a foot in front of her. Neither animal moved and I didn't either, but I could feel my heart beating. The standoff ended when the mouse finally moved and the cat caught it with a swift, clawless swat. The mouse stopped. After a brief moment of stillness, the mouse moved again, the cat met it with another swipe, and once again the mouse stopped. This happened many times. Then the mouse began to back up slowly, and the cat went into a deep crouch and then a mighty pounce. The mouse was trapped between the cat's two paws. It struggled to get away but its efforts were futile, and the cat brought its face close to the mouse, who, in a desperate bid for freedom, bit the cat's nose. The cat's face momentarily recoiled in astonishment. Then the cat's green eyes flashed black like the wing of a crow and her teeth tore into the mouse, and I could hear the tiny bones breaking as the cat's neck swung from side to side until the mouse was still and limp, but the cat's neck continued to swing. Then the cat slung the dead mouse into the short hay and strolled away. This last moment was what surprised and frightened me the most. This whole endeavor had nothing to do with food. And this is when I learned that hardscrabble truth: There is a difference between what a thing is and what it appears to be. A thing can appear to be content and happy as it lies with you so close that you feel its purr in your belly. And if you don't look through the screen door and out into the

world, you might never realize that the thing you think you know and love is another, more dangerous thing altogether.

Once I learned this truth, I began to see examples of it everywhere. A picture hung on the wall of our parlor. In it, a woman was taking a shirt from a clothesline. She had clothespins in her teeth and it was windy and a boy was tugging at her dress. The woman looked like she was in a hurry and the whole scene gave me the idea that, just outside the frame, full, dark clouds were gathering. But that was not what it was.

It was paint.

So I decided right then and there to see the picture as it really was. I stared at the thing long and hard, trying to only see the paint. But it was no use. All my eyes would allow me to see was the lie. In fact, the longer I gazed at the paint, the more false detail I began to imagine. The boy was crying, as if afraid, and the woman was weaker than I had first believed. I finally gave up. I understood then that it takes a powerful imagination to see a thing for what it really is.

That was when I became very interested in magic. A magician can make you believe in appearances even if they are impossible. And, lucky for me, Old Jack was a magician. Also, he was the only one of the old men who paid me any attention. Once I showed my interest in magic, he began to perform his sorcery for me regularly. He could make a penny vanish from his hand and then find it in my ear moments later. He could turn a penny to a nickel and a nickel to a quarter until you couldn't understand why he wasn't the richest man alive. Old Jack could do it all. His tricks amazed me but I knew they weren't real, even at that young age, because I had seen the cat and mouse and thought about the picture in the parlor, so I asked Old Jack to teach me, but he refused. "Can't do that, Sprite. A magician never tells his secrets." But when he said that, it was always with a winking sort of smile, and I understood that one day he would tell me.

Two years passed, and as I grew older I was eager to become a man. On the first Sunday of every month, just before the sun rose, all the men in town would convene at our home to go hunting with my father and my older brother. I wanted to hunt more than anything else, but I was not allowed. In my father's eyes, I wasn't old enough and couldn't be trusted with a gun in the woods, even though I could already hit a can off a fence post with a .22 nine times out of ten. It wasn't fair, but I didn't make the rules, so I had to stay home with the women and Old Jack. Old Jack never went hunting. Not once. Not ever. And the men teased him without mercy, but Old Jack, he'd just smile and say, "Wish I could, boys, but I'm getting behind on my work." But everyone knew that Old Jack was never behind when it came to work.

One Sunday I asked Old Jack straight out why he wouldn't go

hunting, and his answer made me wish I hadn't asked. He said that when he was young he was the best shot in the county and he could shoot a squirrel's eye out at forty feet. And so when he was drafted into the war they made him a sniper. He told me that he had killed and killed for four years, and he said that kind of killing changes a man. He knew they never would have made him kill all those men if he had not learned to shoot so well as a boy. He said when he returned to Canada he felt apart from other men and felt closer to little children, who hadn't yet learned to hate. And I asked Old Jack if he figured he could still shoot a squirrel's eye out at forty feet.

"Don't know," Old Jack said. "I love squirrels now. I've even trained one. I feed him corn right from my hand and he climbs onto my shoulder. Now, that's gotta be kept a secret, Sprite, 'cause if another man found that out, I'm afraid that he would kill my squirrel and dry it on the porch till it was ready to eat."

I knew Old Jack was right about that. The men in our town loved to eat squirrel. "Where's the squirrel, Old Jack?"

"He lives in the toolshed with me; falls asleep right on my belly. I guess I'm the only fellow on this blessed earth who has a squirrel for a pet."

"Will you show him to me, Old Jack?"

"I can't do that, Sprite. He might get spooked and bite you. Maybe I'll just teach you a magic trick instead."

So Old Jack finally showed me how to produce a nickel from behind a boy's ear, and once I knew how it was done, once I knew the trick for what it really was, I became angry. I made Old Jack promise that from now on he would only perform his magic tricks and never tell me the truth behind them.

Things were changing fast for me. The night of my eighth birthday was a night like any other: I was sitting, listening to the men, when Angus Macgregor started talking about the war. I could tell Angus had uncorked the jug early that day. He looked drunk as a boiled owl, and his story didn't make much sense. He said how much he hated the Krauts and that he had once shot a surrendering soldier in the back, and he told us he wasn't sorry for it neither. None of the men said anything for a while after that, and finally my father broke the silence. "I'll get us another round of beers." When I looked over at Old Jack, there was a tear in his eye. I'd never seen that before—a tear in a man's eye. He got up and quietly left the house and I chased after him. When I found him he was sitting under the blighted maple tree.

"You sad, Old Jack? You thinking about the war?" I asked.

Old Jack just sat still for the longest time, like I wasn't even there. It was like he couldn't hear or see me. Like he was hearing and seeing different things. So I just stood there, and after a good long time, Old Jack looked up and seemed surprised that I was in front of him.

"Well, hello, Sprite," he said. "What's the matter? You look kinda down."

"I just didn't like Angus Macgregor's story, that's all."

"Say, Sprite, I know what'll lift your spirits. I know the very thing. How would you like to see a trained squirrel?"

I was very excited. "But you said you could never show him to me, Old Jack."

"I haven't got the money to get you a true birthday present, Sprite. This'll have to do." So we walked down the lane together, toward the north forty. The beneficent moon hung low and shone bright, leading us to the shed. When we arrived there, I was so excited I couldn't wait; I pushed the door open wide and rushed inside, looking for that squirrel, but I couldn't find him. I realized my mistake—that he'd only come out for Old Jack—so I glanced back at the open door, where Old Jack stood, but his back was to me now and it was blocking out the light of the moon. I suddenly remembered that I'd read somewhere how the light of the moon was just an illusion and the moon was only a cold, cold stone. I watched Old Jack look from side to side before he turned his gaze on me, and his eyes flashed black like the wing of a crow. He closed the door and the inside of the shed went black. Then I heard the bolt.

I forget what happened next.

5

EIGHT YEARS OLD
TO THIRTEEN YEARS OLD

forget.

6

THIRTEEN YEARS OLD

Those lost years of mine sure made for a lot of teasing from my family, I'm here to tell you.

"Hey, Norm," my father would say as we ate our supper, "tell us a story from when you were nine. Or ten. Or even twelve. Don't matter which."

And I'd think just as hard as I could, narrowing my eyes and clenching my teeth, anything to try to force a memory to the surface. "Can't remember, Dad," and the whole table would laugh and laugh. And then my father would tell a story about me from that time, a story about me losing a tooth playing hockey, or me dropping a coal-oil lamp in the toolshed and damned near burning it down, or me getting ahold of my father's 12-gauge and shooting six holes into the toolshed like it was some sort of dangerous beast. They would always be great, funny stories and I knew they were true. I had just forgotten them, that's all.

When I finally woke up from my five-year walking sleep, it was as if no time had passed from that moment in the toolshed looking at Old Jack and thinking how his eyes looked like the cat's. The very next moment I was sitting in the back of my father's car with my two brothers. My father was at the wheel and he was telling my mother that when it was his turn, he'd be grateful to go the same way as Old Jack. And my mother agreed and said that the doctor had told her that Old Jack's was the most peaceful death he'd ever witnessed.

When I heard Old Jack's name, I couldn't find my breath and I snatched my older brother's sleeve in a panic, but he just looked annoyed and swatted my hand away.

When we got to Coleman's Funeral Home, Lyle Coleman, the undertaker, was there to meet us. "Is your boy all right, Lloyd?" asked Lyle. I was shaking in an awful way.

"Well, everyone loved Old Jack," my father said. "My middle boy's just more sensitive than most."

"Lloyd, this is the only funeral we've ever had here at Coleman's where there's no family. Surely Old Jack has some kin still alive?"

"Wouldn't know, Lyle," my father said. "All I'm sure of is that for the last twenty years we were Old Jack's family and that's how we'll mourn him."

My brothers were talking and one said to the other, "I've never seen a dead man before. What do you think he'll look like?" And, hearing that, I ran down the dirt road as fast as I could.

My father found me under an old tree that was sick with Dutch elm disease. He sat down and told me that when a man is born, he is born with a great debt, and that one day the debt must be paid. I said that it was unfair, that others should have to pay before Old Jack, but my father explained that the rain falls on all of us, the wicked and the righteous alike. He told me that a man would be judged by his works, and that made me feel better because I knew Old Jack had led a fine and good life. My father told me I had to be strong, that Old Jack would want it that way. I reckoned he was right. So I got up and walked, and my father walked behind me with his right hand on my left shoulder, guiding me back to the funeral home to say goodbye to Old Jack before Lyle Coleman took him under.

The room was filled with folks who talked to each other about Old Jack and what they remembered of him, which wasn't much. He worked hard and he stayed to himself, never complained or had a bad word to say about anyone. The reverend got up and said what a great man Old Jack was, how he had fought bravely in the war and lived the rest of his life serving God and working the fields.

I got in the line with my father and we inched solemnly toward the pine box that would be Old Jack's house from here on in. Suddenly I was next, and fear grabbed my throat and squeezed and I gasped and pulled my tie off. "You okay, son?" my father asked.

"Sure I am," I said, but I was lying. I wasn't okay at all. My brothers were okay, that's for sure, and were already in line to view the body for a second time, as if they were going on a ride at the state fair.

A wild fear seized me: that as soon as I looked into the casket, Old Jack would grab me and pull me into the pine box with him and nobody would see and I would be trapped forever, like a squirrel in a pitch-black shed, a squirrel trained by a magician to perform unspeakable tricks. And then I felt my father's hand gently on my back and I knew it was my turn and I wasn't going to run, so I stepped, alone, to the coffin and looked into it.

And when I looked inside, a curious thought struck me, a thought that made my fear evaporate and my tears dry. You see, Old Jack wasn't lying in the casket; why, it wasn't him at all. It was just something that looked like him, the same way a suit lying on a bed resembles the man once wore it. Old Jack was the best fellow I ever knew and I'd been with him as often as anyone, but I wasn't with him that day, not there in that room, where a line of people stood waiting to look at a thing in a box.

7

DRIVING TO LAS VEGAS

T he stories of my youth are working wonderfully and Adam Eget is awake. Annoyingly awake. He suddenly can't stop talking long enough to shut up about how his girlfriend broke up with him just last week, and how he lost his BlackBerry, which has his sponsor's phone number on it, and how they don't appreciate him enough at The World Famous Comedy Store. And me, I'm riding shotgun, listening to Billy Joe Shaver on the radio and thinking about the plan. I stare out at the black starless night. I only have two hundred dollars to my name, but I have a plan. And the good thing about the plan is that it's foolproof, so I decide I'll get some shuteye now that Adam Eget is exceptionally awake. I close my eyes and turn the car radio way up and Billy Joe Shaver's voice drowns out Adam Eget's—"The Devil made me do it the first time, the second time I done it on my own"—and I smile as I fall asleep.

The slam of the car door wakes me, and my dreams fall away as the facts of my life tumble back into my empty head. I'm alone in the car and look out to see that I'm at the edge of the desert, the Godforsaken desert where the snakes go hungry and die eating dirt. I see that Adam Eget is out there pacing around, agitated, a cigarette stuck to his mouth like always, like they must teach everyone to do at AA. And he's cursing a sky that has no stars, so I ask him what the problem is.

"This is where Kinison died, Norm."

Jesus, if that's true Adam Eget took a detour off Highway 15 that's gonna set us back at least an hour. I get out of the Challenger with the intention of giving Adam Eget a good old-fashioned beating, but then I realize, this is sacred ground, after all. I put one knee down in the hard sand, bow my head, and close my eyes. Sam, the last original voice in comedy, silenced forever when a drunk in a pickup hit him head-on. After the crash, Sam got out of the car, walked around, talked to his best friend, Carl LaBove, and then, finally, to God Himself. He had heard something out there that Carl hadn't, and he seemed at peace with it as he lay down and his spirit rose into the cold desert air. It's sacred ground, all right.

"You knew him, Norm." Adam Eget was kicking the hard sand as if the desert itself was to blame.

I knew him, all right. When I first started out he was real kind to me. Sam wasn't famous yet and couldn't get much work in the States, but Mark Breslin, the fellow who owned all the clubs up in Canada and gave me my start, he wasn't like a regular club owner. He hired Sam when no one else would, and that's how I came to know Sam.

"Did he kill every night, Norm?"

"No. The fact was, he never killed at all. Mark Breslin had a bonus in Sam's contract that Sam would get an extra thousand every time he walked a room. But every single person had to leave. I saw Sam do it twice. Boy, those were crazy days, Adam Eget, crazy beautiful days."

"Why didn't he kill?"

"How do I know? Truth was, it was a mystery, because he could shake a room to its foundations and the folks knew that something was going on, but they'd get up and leave just the same. Maybe folks don't want anything new; maybe they just want to hear the things they already know. How the hell should I know?"

"What was he like before he was famous, Norm?"

"Oh, he was a sight to see. The rest of us, we all dressed in suit jackets and shoes like our dads wore, but Sam's jacket was a long duster, and he always wore a bandana too. And when he talked, it was a wild shriek, but there was music in it. It put me in mind of a Pentecostal minister I'd seen once who hailed from West Texas and came up through the Ottawa Valley when I was a young boy— a man who handled snakes and talked unafraid. Sam put me in mind of him, and for good reason too. Turned out Sam used to be a preacher himself. Anyway, I was just starting out in comedy at the time, and Sam came through Ottawa and he took a liking to me. So he let me travel with him and open for him all across Canada."

"I bet you have good stories about Sam, don't you, Norm?"

"Oh, sure. I remember one time we were flying from Toronto to Winnipeg, Sam and I, and before we took off the captain came over the intercom, as is the custom on airplanes. 'Good morning,' the captain said. 'This is your captain, Pat Johnson, and we will be flying—' and Sam gave out a wild scream: 'NOOOOOO!!!!! NOT CRASH JOHNSON! NOT CRASH JOHNSON!!!!!!!!! AAAAAAAAAAAAAHHHHHHHH!!!!!!!!!' Well, it was about the funniest thing I'd ever heard, the idea that this captain had been in so many accidents that his nickname was Crash. That just busted me up and I started laughing and couldn't stop. Of course, nobody else found it funny at all—it caused quite an alarm—and Sam got himself a good talking-to by the girls that bring you the little drinks, but he didn't care. He had me laughing hard, which I guess was the only thing he was after. He apologized to the girls, giggling the whole time. You know, that old Sam giggle."

"Yeah," says Adam Eget. "I really wish I'd met him, but it was before my time. There are so many great Kinison stories at the Store. It's so unfair that guys like Sam have to die so young and a sonofa-bitch like Nelson Mandela lived to be an old man."

"Nelson Mandela wasn't a sonofabitch. He fought apartheid and they put him in prison for more than twenty years. And when they finally released him and he took power, he never exacted revenge on his enemies. Instead, he exacted forgiveness on them and brought his torn nation together."

"I thought he stole some diamonds."

"No."

"Didn't he steal a bunch of diamonds and then sell them back to the guy he stole them from?"

"No."

"Who am I thinking of, then?"

"Don't know. Let's get back in the car now. It's cold in the desert."

I don't like it in the middle of the desert late at night. I know this is when the creatures emerge. They spend their days hiding from the merciless sun behind rocks and cactus, and it's when the sun goes down that they make their living. In the black of night I can hear them, hungry, scrabbling over the rocks. And I look over at Adam Eget but he's looking down, lost, the way a man looks when there's nothing but darkness around him and the only thing that will help is a deep, deep swig from a bottle. Of course, Adam Eget lost the bottle five years ago and now he has nothing. It makes me feel bad, sorta.

"C'mon, Adam Eget, let's move. We'll stop at the border, at Whiskey Pete's, and we'll eat fried bread and molasses while I tell you the plan. How does that sound to you?"

"You'll tell me the plan, Norm? You'll tell me what this is all about?"

"Yeah, sure I will. If you want to know it, I'll tell it to you."

"I want to know, Norm. I want to know the plan."

That makes me laugh. I don't dare fall asleep in the car now. Adam Eget looks seriously unnerved, and the highway from L.A. to Vegas is scarred every few miles by black rubber—the last evidence of tumbling, burning cars. But I'm the passenger and my job is to keep the driver relaxed and happy, and that means telling him more stories. Stories from the old days.

8

STARTING OUT

"**Y**ou got boots?!"

I suppose I had heard that line from Charlie a hundred times. He never looked up at me, though, so I don't think he ever saw my face.

"Yes, sir, I got boots."

I'd take a seat with the rest of the boys in the middle of the room and we'd play euchre or hearts—nothing too hard. I was convinced some of the boys, like Billy Saunders, weren't there for a day's work at all but just wanted company. I never heard the sound of Billy's boots hitting the floor when Charlie called out a job for the day. That was all right, though. More work for me.

I specialized in unskilled labor, and I was good at it. Skilled labor appealed to a different sort. It was for the thinking men. Men who liked to use their heads as much as their bodies. I didn't like to use my head, but I loved unskilled, manual labor. That kind of work let my mind alone, let it be free. If my job was to shovel and shovel until eight hours had passed, then my body worked on its own. It had no use for my mind. So my mind would take off to a world of imagination. And that's where stand-up comedy started.

One morning I sat at the card table with the boys and told them a funny idea that had come to my idle mind as my body had been busy at the jackhammer. It concerned answering machines, and everybody around the table got a big laugh from it. From then on, as I worked I would let my mind flow toward a comic place, committed to making the boys at the card table laugh the next day.

I was twenty-one in 1984 when Mark Breslin opened Yuk Yuk's comedy club in Ottawa. I was making $21.20 a day for Charlie, and Mark was offering fifteen dollars a set. A set took about five minutes and you could do two a night if you were lucky, so the decision was pretty easy. And never once did Mark Breslin ask me if I had boots.

Mark owned branches of Yuk Yuk's all across Canada, and Howie Wagman was, and still is, the manager of the Ottawa club. Howie helped me with the ins and outs of comedy. I'll never forget my first line on a stand-up stage. "How many of you guys own answering machines?" To this day it remains one of my strongest lines.

I quickly developed a cult following. That sounds pretty good, but the truth is that it's the last thing you want to develop. The only time having a cult following is a great thing is when you are actually in a cult. Then you get to be a cult leader and life is milk and honey. First off, everyone thinks you are God, so you get to tell them all what to do. Your followers bow down before you and give you all their worldly goods, which can really add up, even with a smallish cult. The best part is you get to lie down with all the ladies from the cult, even the married ones. In a short matter of time, you become drunk with power and begin to lie down with the men also, not because you want to, but just because you can. Yes, being a cult leader with a cult following is fine work if you can find it.

However, being a stand-up comedian with a cult following just means that most folks hate your guts.

9

MY GREATEST GIG

"Tell me another story, Norm! Tell me about the greatest gig you ever did."

"That's easy, Adam Eget."

A comedian never forgets his greatest gig. But the details slip away with time. And the Devil is in the details and so is God. So I pick up a brand-new syrette and fill it with grains and grains of morphine and puncture the flesh between my middle and ring finger. I give myself a large dose because this memory is long in the past. When the drug hits hard, the present is gone along with the white Challenger, but there's a red Datsun in its place. It is 1985 and I am a young man who's done stand-up for only a year and I'm driving to a gig, all by myself. The beautiful opioid allows me to see this all as if it happened yesterday and not ten thousand yesterdays ago.

I had gotten a gig doing comedy at a hospital, for the patients. It didn't pay any money, but that's not why a comic does a gig like that. You take that type of gig just because you want to be a good person and receive eternal life.

Sonofabitch, the drive was long. Why they built a hospital so damn far away from everybody, I couldn't figure. It was way out in the middle of northern Ontario, where you have to pray your car doesn't break down, and if it does, you have to pray you freeze to death before the timberwolves find you. Well, the people who built it must have known what they were doing. After all, they owned a hospital and I was just some guy in a car asking questions to myself. Suddenly, in the middle of nothing, where the infinite nothing of the sky meets the infinite nothing of the snow, I saw something. It was a small square blue sign—a sign indicating a hospital ahead. It may as well have read, LAST CHANCE FOR HEART ATTACK FOR 300 MILES.

I was getting close and getting nervous too. Maybe it was the barbed wire around the perimeter or maybe it was the armed guards. What kind of hospital was I playing, anyway? I got my answer quick enough, because it was written on a big sign: HOSPITAL FOR THE CRIMINALLY INSANE. My agent had never been big on details.

It took me a while just to get into the place. First they patted me down and took all my weapons and my drugs. Then they looked up my ass and took those weapons and those drugs as well. But finally they let me go from the outside to the inside.

"Take me to the warden," I demanded.

"This is a hospital, son; there's no warden."

"Fine, then take me to the entertainment director!"

We walked down a long corridor filled with howls of anguish and high wailing screeches.

Every cage I passed had a guy in it, and every guy was acting odder than the last. The first guy was scratching his hair real hard even though it was shorn close, like he was trying to scratch inside his head or something, and he just kept saying, "I was at John D. Rockefeller's funeral." Then the next guy was just staring at me, stone still, and he had a big smile on his lips but his eyes were cold dead. I started laughing to beat hell.

"How do you work with these characters all day and not crack up?" I asked the orderly.

"Oh, you get used to it."

"What about the guy with the cold dead eyes standing there?" I asked. "What'd he do to get in here?"

"Oh, his name's Fred Henshaw. He took his mother out to the cold northern tundra where the sun never sets and he cut off her eyelids. That way she couldn't sleep or even shield her eyes from the sun. Then Fred had her wander around, tripping in the snow, falling, getting back up, falling again. Every day Fred would take a hypodermic needle and remove a half a pint of blood from the old lady. After about a week, his mother just lay down on the hard snow. Then he sat down and waited. Waited for the crows to come."

"Oh my God, that's the worst thing I've ever heard of. What about the guy before him, Mr. Itchyhead—what did he do?"

"Oh, him? Trust me, you don't want to know."

These characters' shenanigans became less amusing after I heard their backstories. I was starting to get real nervous about the show, thinking that maybe these guys wouldn't be able to relate to my material. How could they be expected to understand the difference between cats and dogs or the difference between Los Angeles and New York if they didn't understand the difference between right and wrong?

I was shown into a room, where I met the entertainment director. "Listen, pal, I wanna do good and all, but I think this is a big mistake. When I heard this was a hospital, I imagined sick people, really sick people, the kind you want nothing to do with. Some of these fellows look healthier than you and me."

"Oh, don't worry, you'll do fine. We had the Gatlin Brothers last week."

The Gatlin Brothers? I couldn't believe my ears. But then the guy showed me the room and it was world class, with steep stadium seating and perfect acoustics. I'd only seen such a fancy venue one time, and that was for a crowd made up of folks who'd never slaughtered a single man. It was like a broken calculator. It just didn't add up. "How is it these monsters deserve such a fancy venue?"

"Well, let me explain something, Norm. You see, technically, all these fellows are not guilty. Not guilty by reason of insanity. Do you understand?"

"No."

"Every one of these men has been found not guilty in the eyes of the law."

"Oh."

Well, that shed a different light on the situation. If these guys weren't guilty of anything, then they deserved the best show I could give them. I guess I always kinda knew that deep down, but it took the entertainment director to make me realize it.

Soon showtime arrived and I stood in the wings, peering through the curtains. The room was made to hold about five hundred, but I could see there were only roughly seven people assembled.

"Where is everybody?"

The entertainment director shook his head. "I can't figure it. There's not a single other form of diversion in this entire hospital for the criminally insane." And then he looked at me mean, like it was my fault.

"It's not my fault," I said.

"When we had the Gatlin Brothers last week, we had to turn people away. Criminally insane people. It broke my heart. Well, get out there, you're on." And he pushed me toward the stage, really hard.

I hit the stage to silence. "Good evening, folks. How many of you here own an answering machine?"

"None of us, that's how many," answered one, and the other six grumbled in assent.

"You got any complaints, Tuesday morning meeting's the time to bring 'em up, Kowalski, you know that. Now, pipe down and let the man speak," said a guard.

"Anyhow," I continued, "I got one, and they're more trouble

than they're worth, in many ways. Now, say a man phones you and . . ." I just couldn't go on.

One of the criminally insane men had found his way onto the stage and had begun biting my leg hard, and the guard had begun striking him with the business end of a baton, but that just caused the criminally insane man to dig his teeth in deeper. I started shrieking, and the audience got a big kick out of that, so the other patients began to wander into the auditorium to see what the commotion was, and by the time they finally shed my leg of the criminally insane man's teeth, the place was full, with everybody clapping and cheering and biting.

It was the greatest show I ever had.

10

STAR SEARCH

Star Search was a show where they searched for stars. The show had different categories such as junior dancers, spokespersons, singers, and comedians. Once a year they would do a special *International Star Search*, where they would gather up a bunch of foreigners and try to make them stars. That's why they contacted me. I was a foreigner. The good news was, if I won, I'd go from a nobody to a star.

Sam Kinison had told Dennis Miller about me—told him I was international—and Dennis, who is a very generous man, helped me, as he would many times in my career. Dennis passed my information on to the show's host, Ed McMahon.

Ed was famous for sitting beside Johnny Carson and laughing his deep, genuine laugh at all that Johnny uttered. If you're the best at something, you become a rich man. And Ed McMahon was very rich.

The show had four judges, one of whom was Robin Leach. The

judges would judge you by giving you between one and four stars. These stars would be added together and divided by four, to yield your score. So if you were awarded four stars—that was the perfect score—that meant each of the judges gave you four stars, which I was pretty sure I would receive.

I was backstage with my agent and a bunch of dirty foreigners. I was one of them, but only technically, because I was from Canada. In Canada, everything we watch on TV and buy in stores is American, and also we speak the same language. I never *felt* like I was in a different country when I was in the United States.

My opponent's name was the Bushman. He was very funny, and backstage he had us all in stitches. He was from Africa and wore a multicolored tribal robe with a matching hat. He couldn't have looked more out of place in America, and I couldn't have looked more in place. At first I thought this gave me an enormous advantage, but then I had a second thought.

Perhaps this out-of-placeness would actually work in the Bushman's favor. After all, this was *International Star Search,* and Canada was well known as the least international of all countries. My other problem was that none of my jokes were remotely international. Every one of them dealt with a domestic issue of the United States of America. I told my agent I felt I was in big trouble, and he told me that I was being ridiculous, that I was sure to win. My agent often told me something positive like this right before a catastrophe happened. I was backstage in a room we all shared and I was hungry, but there was nothing to eat, because many of the performers hailed from third-world countries and had either ravenously devoured the food or placed it in their pockets. I struck up a conversation with a couple of Nicaraguan junior dancers, who were adorably cute but who began circling me in a way that had me patting my back pocket to see if my wallet was still there.

Things were making me extremely agitated, and that can be very bad for a performer. I decided to go outside and go through my pre-show ritual.

Since I started stand-up, I have used the following pre-show ritual as a way of controlling my nerves and centering myself. First I close my eyes and take a deep breath. Then I create a picture in my mind. It is always the same picture. I am lying in a glade near a brook while a gentle breeze licks my face and makes me smile. Birds fill the sky with song as I lounge beside the brook with my golden Lab and watch the fish as they jump out of the water and back in again. I walk leisurely to the water and take a long, deep drink of it, and it is always clean and cold and slakes my thirst. Then I lie down again on the grass and let my golden Lab lick my face, and then I wrestle with him and laugh. Then I open my eyes. This part of the ritual takes about fifteen minutes. It never fails to clear my mind, as an eraser clears a busy chalkboard.

Then it is time for my body. I stretch, beginning with my calves, and then, without hurry, add to the stretch so that it spreads all the way up my body and finishes with the neck. This is crucial, since I hold most of my stress in my neck. I make sure each stretch is slow and deliberate, and as I perform the stretches I listen through headphones to the calming strumming of the zither, the most relaxing of all musical instruments. With my mind in a state of cheerful slack and my body loosed, it is then time to work on my soul. I take out six two-milligram bars of Xanax and slowly swallow them. Then I reach into my back pocket to find my flask, which is always filled with Wild Turkey 101. I upend it into my mouth and drink until I have to stop to gasp for breath. Then I vomit. Then I close my eyes again and think about the dog and the stream and all that shit. Then I end my pre-show routine by punching my agent in the stomach.

If you want to become a performer in show business—and that includes modern dance—I strongly advise this pre-show ritual.

I was instructed that on *International Star Search* I was to perform for two minutes, not a second more or a second less. To make sure I stuck to my time, there was a large digital clock in front of me that counted down from two minutes to zero. Whenever I performed my stand-up, I had one ironclad rule: I always made sure to begin with my strongest joke, my surefire laugh-getter, my answering-machine joke, and so I came right out with it. It got no laughs.

This was a big problem. When I had chosen my two minutes of material, I had taken into account the laughter of the audience. But there was a complete absence of laughter, and as I completed my final joke I saw, in horror, I still had a minute and fifteen seconds left to perform. I was sweating hard and my throat was as dry as kindling. I could hear dangerous mutterings from the crowd, much of it in a foreign tongue, and I looked over in a panic to Ed McMahon, who was also not laughing, unless you consider an angry glare a type of laughter. Ed McMahon, the man whose job was to laugh. Ed McMahon, who was put on this earth to laugh. Ed McMahon, who was paid exorbitant amounts of money to laugh. Ed McMahon was not laughing.

But I was a pro and I still had a little over a minute to win the crowd back. That's the beauty of stand-up comedy. One moment the audience may hate you and the next you are on its shoulders. I looked out at them. "So, you're saying you don't have an answering machine? None of you? I find that very hard to believe. I think you are liars, and I implore the judges to ignore the boos and jeers and hisses that are filling this auditorium and drowning out my voice. These people are filthy foreigners and wouldn't know funny if it bit them in the ass. Show some guts, for once in your life, and don't be swayed by this transatlantic mob. Robin Leach, I'm sure you have an answering machine and agreed on many of the points I have made tonight."

I had plenty more to say but my time came to an end, so I trundled offstage, where I encountered a very confident Bushman and I wished him luck.

My agent was in the wings. "I thought it went great!" he said.

"What? They never laughed. Not once."

"You don't understand. You're used to clubs and this is TV. The studio audience never laughs, because they are too intimidated.

These things are all sweetened in the editing. Trust me, I've been at this awhile and . . ."

I didn't hear anything else my agent said, because the Bushman had done his first joke, and the audience laughed loudly for two straight minutes. When the Bushman exited, walking past us, my agent stopped explaining to me how studio audiences never laugh at anything and ran down the hall, business card in hand, calling out to the Bushman.

Now, usually after a bad set, you can just leave and buy yourself a steak and a woman and forget the whole thing, but on this show you had to wait until the end, when they announced the winners in all the categories. I wandered around and saw the Nicaraguan junior dancer team, who must have had a bad set too, judging by the way they were sobbing. I told the mother that they should stop, but she explained that her family was very poor and this was their ticket out of the slums of Managua but that her son had dropped his sister during their routine and now their dream was dead. I told her not to worry, that there was no such thing as a junior dancer in real life, that it only existed on this one television show, so it was all for naught, anyway. What's more, I said, not a single thing in life mattered. That seemed to cheer the mother up.

It was finally time for me to go back onstage. First the international spokesmen were judged, then the international singers. Then it was time for the comedians. I walked out with the Bushman and we received a standing ovation as well as a chorus of boos. Never had I felt so much hate for me mixed with so much love for someone other than me.

Ed read from the teleprompter: "And now in the comedy division, another hard decision for the judges."

This brought the house down. I've been in comedy for a while, but I don't think I've ever heard a bigger laugh, before or since. Ed did his best not to join in the laughter—I gotta give it to him—and he continued on.

"The Bushman receives . . . FOUR STARS." The perfect score. Each judge had given him four stars.

"And Norm Macdonald receives . . . THREE QUARTERS OF A STAR."

I could not believe it. As I left the stage I did the math. It meant that three of the judges had given me one star and one judge had given me zero stars, and I bet dollars to donuts it was that sonofabitchofaRobinLeach.

11

THE PLAN

Adam Eget and I sit across from each other in a red plastic booth at the coffee shop in Whiskey Pete's. Now, Whiskey Pete's is a small casino that sits in a small town called Primm, right at the border of California and Nevada, and it's designed for people who can't wait the extra ninety minutes to feed the gamble in their gut. The stakes are low and the tables are dingy. Every time I'm here, I wonder if some tourist from a faraway land has ever flown into L.A., rented a car, and was on his way to Vegas when the poor bastard saw Primm and Whiskey Pete's and the other coupla casinos and the water parks, and he figured it must be Las Vegas, the oasis in the desert. So he just stayed there the whole week, and when he returned to his faraway home, he told everyone about Las Vegas and how disappointing it was. It has to have happened.

Adam Eget and I eat fried bread and molasses and the waiter says he knows me from somewhere. I point to my hat. "No," he says. I point to my jacket. "No," he says. I point to my shirt. "No," he says.

"Aren't you the fellow who lives at Sullivan's Boarding House, down near the Nickel, in Los Angeles? I knew you two years ago and you still owe me a sawbuck."

"Fine," I say, and pay him the ten bucks. Then I tell him to get us a fresh pot of coffee and start to tell Adam Eget my plan. I guess I can't in all honesty call it my plan, on account of the way it came to me all at once without thinking. I was just standing onstage at The World Famous Comedy Store, getting no laughs, when a picture brightened my mind. It was as if another man's well-thought-out plan had been magically planted in my head.

"This is the plan, Adam Eget. As you know I have no money, I am as broke as Christ Himself, and this is because I've lost all my money. I've lost all my money on games of chance. But it has come to me that losing all this money has given me something just as valuable."

Adam Eget looks puzzled. "What is as valuable as money?"

I pause and look him in the eye. I want him to understand the plan the first time so I don't have to repeat it over and over again and field all manner of follow-up questions. "Good credit, that's what. Debts paid, that's what. I've always paid off my markers, so I have very good credit. And when you don't owe the casino, in a funny way, the casino owes you."

"I don't follow," says Adam Eget, as he smokes a Marlboro Red and fills his mouth with fried bread and molasses.

"That's the way it works in Las Vegas. You pay your markers promptly and you build up trust. See, Vegas works on odds. If you've always lost and paid your markers, odds say you'll just keep on doing the same thing."

Adam Eget nods. "I got you. Sure." But his eyes are dim as dusk and I know he still doesn't follow.

"I don't have but two hundred dollars to my name, but Las Vegas doesn't know that. I've got a line of credit with the biggest casinos in the city. Between the Mirage, Harrah's, Caesars, and the Horseshoe, I have over a million dollars in credit."

Adam Eget's eyes become marginally less dim. "So we get these casinos to lend you the million, but then we don't gamble with it. We take a powder and drive straight north to Old Mexico!" He farts loudly.

"No, Adam Eget, the casinos give you chips and you can only use them to gamble, and if you win, you must pay off your markers and can only keep your winnings."

Adam Eget smiles and nods wisely, and when he does, molasses drips slowly down onto his chin and then begins to harden. "So, the plan is to win, then."

"Well, sure, that's always the plan. But this time it's only Plan A. You see, I have a Plan B. I've never had a Plan B before, but this time I do."

Adam Eget puts what is left of his cigarette into his mouth, but it is very short now and a full third of it is orange ember. He tries to pull the cigarette from his mouth, but it is stuck to his molasses-covered lips, so instead his fingers slide down and fix upon the ember. It takes him a considerably longer time to feel the pain than a smarter man would take, but when he does, he jumps to his feet and yelps loudly. He digs at the ember embedded in his thumb until it finally dislodges. "Sonofabitchbastard," he shouts, and an uproar of laughter fills the coffee shop at Whiskey Pete's. Adam Eget finishes his fine burlesque with a stupid smile to the laughing patrons.

I wait with the patience of Job.

"Plan A, I bet my million until I have a million in profit, then I quit gambling forever. I quit everything. I'm a certified, genuine millionaire. I buy a ranch in Montana, and sit on my porch all day, and drink Wild Turkey 101, and watch other men work for me."

"That sounds like heaven," Adam Eget says, one hand on his sore lip, the other in a glass of ice water.

"Yes," I say, "but a heaven where I am God, and the men who work for me are men."

"What is Plan B?" says Adam Eget.

"Plan B is to lose the entire million." I study Adam Eget's face for a reaction to my provocative comment, but then I see in his eyes that a delayed, more powerful wave of pain is hitting his small brain.

"Owwwwwwwwwwwwwww!" he screams, and the coffee shop explodes in laughter once again as Adam Eget jumps to his feet and begins to dance from table to table.

I wait again. I have the patience of Job. And when he's finally done, I tell him the rest of Plan B.

"Have you ever heard of a script doctor, Adam Eget?"

"Sure, Norm. Those are those smart fellows from Harvard who punch up screenplays to make them funnier."

I laugh at the innocence. "You've been living in Hollywood too long. The real script doctors sell magic. Not cheap, not cheap at all. There's a drug named Dilaudid. It costs ten thousand dollars. A small dose proves lethal. I have a friend in Vegas named Gabe, who knows a script doctor who can provide me with this drug. If I lose, I simply put it in my blood, say my prayers, lay down, and die in my free bed."

"So that's Plan B, huh?"

"Yes, and when I get to heaven I tell God that I died better than broke. In my last act, I stole a million dollars from some of the Devil's boys. I figure that oughta impress God just fine."

"So either way you win."

"That's the idea." I can tell it's finally sinking in.

"Where do I fit in?"

"If I win, you become my head ranch hand and make five percent more money than the other ranch hands and get beaten far less often."

"Sounds good." Adam Eget beams. "Do I get my own horse?"

"No."

"But what if you lose and kill yourself? Then where do I fit in?"

I guess that would hurt most men—a guy you've known for twenty years asking what he gets when you toss away your soul in a Las Vegas hotel room—but I understand the ways of men, all right.

Everybody's in it for himself. Adam Eget's just like everyone else. And my Plan B also takes care of him after I murder myself in cold blood.

"You're the one who finds me dead, and you cry and shake like a little girl, the way you just did a minute ago. Then later you write a book about me and they pay you money."

"But I can't write. I'm not smart enough."

"Don't worry about that, Adam Eget. For idiots like you, they provide a ghostwriter. A ghostwriter is a man blessed with bright talent but cursed with dim luck. The brilliant ghostwriter will do all the work and receive a pittance, while you, an illiterate fool, will be given a king's ransom. That's God's great joke, my son."

My name's Keane. I'm a ghostwriter. Nothing you have read in this book has been written by Mr. Macdonald. That is my job, to write these sorts of books for these sorts of people. But this one I was excited about. I was a very, very big fan of Norm Macdonald.

Was.

12

ME, GABE VELTRI, AND A SQUID

Like all ugly things, Fremont Street is uglier when the sun is bright. This Saturday noon it is scorchingly ugly.

"Why are we downtown?" whines Adam Eget.

"You'll see," I say, reaching over to lean on the horn. A moment later a man emerges from an apartment building and walks briskly toward us. The man is Gabe Veltri, a professional poker player. He makes a fine living at the Aria poker room playing limit hold 'em, where he joylessly books his sixty hours a week. When the market tumbled a few years back, Gabe went bottom-feeding and snatched up a property here on Fremont Street, where the hustlers and whores beg and cajole. When he's in Vegas this is his home, except for the times I'm in town, and then he stays with me in my comped suite.

What I like about Gabe is there's no gamble in him. We walked by a roulette table at Caesars one time, and when I asked Gabe to guess the number he said, "Twenty-six," and the wheel spun and, lo and behold, the little silver ball landed on 26. We hadn't placed a bet, but the table had heard his guess and everybody was going nuts.

I said, "Gabe, how much do you wish you'd bet a grand on twenty-six?"

"Not at all," he said, and kept walking. Now, that's rare, and I'll tell you what's even rarer. I've never heard Gabe tell that story. It's not even a story to him. Gabe is just the kind of wingman a guy like me will need for my plan to succeed. Gabe will keep me grounded. He'll shame me so I stay away from the pits. I've decided I'll only bet sports and that I won't go near the tables, where the serpents lie in coil to offer me free meals and free rooms and other expensive things. This will allow me the time I need to properly handicap the day's games. I decide to bet mostly on baseball, because baseball is the easiest sport to predict.

Why did I insist on Adam Eget coming along on this trip? It's not 'cause he's a friend. My plan has no place for friends. It's not because of his pretty green eyes either. The fact is that Adam Eget, the dolt's dolt, possesses a particular type of magic. Adam Eget knows nothing about sports and will often say things like, "Why do different baseball teams wear different uniforms? That doesn't seem fair," or, "Why do they call it a hockey stick, anyways?" But Adam Eget can pick winners. Out of the blue, he'll go into a sort of a trance and then, the way a robot might, he'll suddenly pronounce, "The New York Rangers will win their hockey match tonight," or, "The Indianapolis Colts will win their football match tonight," and he'll have me scrambling to call my bookie. The problem is, he does this type of thing very rarely and without warning. But when he does, he is always right. Always. He's like that squid that picks the winner of the World Cup once every four years. He is very good at exactly one thing. The rest of the time Adam Eget is just a stupid squid.

Gabe slides into the backseat of the Challenger.

"Gabe, Adam Eget, Gabe."

With pleasantries taken care of, it is time to be on our way. "Listen, boys, before we hit the Strip, whaddya say we go to the El Cortez and get some fried bread?"

The fellows think this is a capital idea and so we go and eat breakfast and talk, like civilized gentlemen in the middle of this jungle of vipers.

I notice as we drink our coffee that Adam Eget's eyes are not on Gabe or on me. He is looking beyond us, somewhere in the middle distance. I just assume he is gazing at his bleak and certain future. But, no, I turn my head and see he is staring at a lady who is waiting to be seated. She is dressed sexy as hell, in a tight dress and high heels. "Fellas," Adam Eget says, "I think I'll go and introduce myself to the future Mrs. Adam Eget."

I wish him good luck and watch as he approaches her, as he offers her a cigarette, as he stands too close to her, but she doesn't seem to mind.

"Wonder if he'll close the deal. What are the odds, Gabe?"

Gabe hasn't been paying attention, as the fried bread and molasses has arrived, but he looks over and studies the pair closely.

"Well, Norm, to answer your question, I'd say the odds are good, but the goods are odd."

"No way. Seriously, Gabe, you think that's a dude?"

"Look at the way she dresses and talks and moves. You ever see a lady act that sexy?"

Gabe is right. Only dudes act as sexy as this lady. "I better go warn Adam Eget."

But it's too late. They are gone.

Gabe and I head over to the Mirage. It makes me feel strong as I walk the floor and easily pass the blackjack and craps tables, feeling no pull. It helps to have Gabe beside me, knowing that if I stop at a table he'll call me a jackass. When we get to my suite, I pull out my laptop and scour the baseball standings to find any trends. I'll be up early the next day to see the Pinnacle lines. Pinnacle is an offshore betting site that always has truer odds than Vegas. Information is everything. I am proud to see that Gabe is proud of me.

Gabe tosses me the drugs. "So, I'm interested to hear a plan that needs 10K worth of Dilaudid."

"I'm trying to play smart this time, Gabe. You see, I'm playing for my life. And if I win, I'm a millionaire." I take out the syrettes and the brochures from Montana and explain my plan.

Gabe looks at me for a long time and then smiles. "So, you bet a million and you either win a million or lose everything, including your life. It's double or nothing. I like it." Double or nothing. Only Gabe would think of it that way, and we laugh together at whatever it is men laugh at when all else is lost.

We order way too much room service, which is what men do when food is comped, and as soon as we hang up the phone there's a knock on the door and one of us says, "That was fast," which is what men say when that happens.

It is Adam Eget.

"Hey, why didn't you phone?"

"I told you, I lost my BlackBerry, remember? It has my sponsor's number on it. But I didn't drink. One day at a time, right?"

"Right, right. I thought you'd end up at one of those tiny chapels with some Elvis impersonator marrying you and that dude," I say.

"That was no dude. Her name was Sammi, with an 'i,' and she was crazy in the sack. Real aggressive."

"Whatever. Get yourself a soda while we wait for the room service."

"Oh, thanks, I will. But she's definitely not a dude."

"Look at the coffee table and tell me what you see, Adam Eget."

"It's a wineglass full of nickels."

"That's right. You will use those nickels to play your favorite game."

Adam Eget's face lights up like a child's birthday cake. "Video keno?"

"Yes, video keno. But first you use a few of the nickels to buy the *Las Vegas Review-Journal* and look at the sports lines, and if you find a winner you tell me, okay?"

"Sure, boss, sure. I'll start right now."

So Adam Eget goes and returns with a newspaper and scans the next day's lines, but he falls into no trance and finally grows tired of it and turns to the funny pages to read *Marmaduke,* and he laughs really hard. Then he sees the food that's arrived in his absence and fills his face with shrimp and steak. He eats fast, like gluttons do, and much of the food spills from his mouth and falls to his shirt. Gabe is on his iPad, running simulations of something, and I lie back on the couch and take stock of myself. I feel great excitement at what lies ahead. The enormity of the stakes, the idea of a game being played for life and death, does not sober me but instead does the opposite. I feel drunk with confidence. A simple piece of logic convinces me I will win. I cannot conceive of my own death, and since a loss would result in such, it follows that I cannot conceive of my own loss. My father passed away many years before my gambling compulsion was born. He would not have approved. Every Sunday when I was a boy, my aunt Laura would buy a lottery ticket, always making sure she used the identical numbers. The ticket only cost a dollar, but my father called it foolishness and often counseled my aunt to quit this habit. One Sunday, my aunt was over for dinner, and as we were finishing dessert she jumped from her chair. "Oh, my goodness, I almost forgot to get my ticket. I'd better go before Barkley's closes."

"Oh, why don't you skip it this week, Laura?" my dad said.

"But I can't," said my aunt. "They're my lucky numbers. What if I were to skip this week and my lucky numbers hit?"

My dad wiped some gravy from his lips and looked at his sister. "Well, Laura, if that were to happen, I would say they were not your lucky numbers. I would say they were your unlucky numbers."

I busted a gut at that one.

I look over at Gabe and think he would have liked my dad. Gabe always tells me, "Luck is for losers." I plan to keep this firmly in my mind whenever I feel lucky, whenever I feel I can beat a dealer or a croupier. The money will all come from the Sports Book. I know that with patience and research, I can beat the odds.

After all, I had beat the odds before, again and again. For blackjack or baccarat or roulette, you need exceedingly good luck but nowhere near the luck it takes to succeed in show business without a shred of talent. So I sit the boys down and explain to them how a punk doing stand-up comedy in Canada decided to go to Hollywood and roll the dice on Mr. Johnny Carson.

13

THE TONIGHT SHOW STARRING
JOHNNY CARSON

Adam Eget has pity all over his face and in his stupid voice.

"But I thought you already went to Hollywood to go on that show where they search for stars. But you lost. Just imagine if you had won!"

"Well, it's like that expression, Adam Eget. Everything happens for a reason."

"I've never heard that expression."

"You haven't? It's a very, very famous and popular expression. Women are particularly fond of it."

"I don't even know what it means," says Adam Eget. "So everything happens for a reason? I never knew. Everything happens for a reason. . . . So there's some secret reason I ate that bowl of Frankenberries for breakfast."

"You know something? You make it hard to tell a story, but I will go on. As I was saying, everything happens for a reason," I say, and then I tell my story.

*   *   *

After my *Star Search* debacle I stayed in Los Angeles and worked at the Improv, The World Famous Comedy Store, and the Laugh Factory. I had decided to take a break from the road to try to perfect my material at the L.A. clubs. Every night I went onstage and afterward I hung out and talked to the audience, answering their questions, which were always the same: "What is the Bushman like in real life?" "Do you think the Bushman will come here tonight?" "If the Bushman does come here tonight, would you mind taking a picture of him with me?"

I met some great comics in Los Angeles, and the best one, and the one who became my friend and hero, was Rodney Dangerfield. Many a night I sat at the back of the Improv, watching Rodney the way a dog watches a man, or a man a god. This guy was the complete package. He looked funny, he talked funny, he even moved funny—tugging at his tie and wiping sweat off his brow—and all the while his comically bulging eyes shifted nervously from side to side. He wrote the best jokes any comic has ever written. But that's news to nobody.

I know another side of Rodney.

I've got the inside scoop on big-time celebrities, and one of them is Rodney Dangerfield. Soon after meeting Rodney, when he was at the peak of his career, I learned a very distressing truth. And that truth was that success and money mean nothing when it comes to achieving happiness.

From an outsider's perspective, it seemed Rodney had everything: money, success, fame. But there was one thing Rodney Dangerfield was never able to attain, and it plagued him his entire life. The ugly little secret in Hollywood was that Rodney Dangerfield never got any respect.

Now, I know that's hard to believe, but hear me out. Every story Mr. Dangerfield told me was more heartbreaking than the last. It had all started when he was a child and his father told him that his dying wish was to have little Rodney sit on his lap. I thought it was such an adorable thing for a father to tell his son. I really did. Until Rodney informed me his dad was sitting in the electric chair at the time.

Rodney's mother now had to raise the boy alone and decided to get him a dog, but she didn't think the dog would play with a tot such as Rodney unless she tied a pork chop around the boy's neck.

Rodney finally grew up and became a man, but things didn't improve. One time, he recalled, a hooker informed him, "Not tonight, I have a headache." Imagine hearing that from a prostitute.

I told Rodney that when I felt the whole world was against me, I'd find a tavern, where a bartender would always lend an understanding ear. But Rodney said he tried that once and that when he asked the bartender for a double, the bartender brought out a guy who looked just like Rodney.

Rodney told me story after story and each had an identical theme: Rodney Dangerfield, famous, wealthy comedy superstar, just didn't get any respect, no respect at all. Are you kidding me?

I suggested a therapist, and a sad look came into Rodney's rheumy eyes. He had seen one, yes, and the therapist—and I use the term very loosely—said Rodney was crazy. Rodney demanded a second opinion, and the cruel psychiatrist told him that he was ugly as well. I felt so bad for my friend and hero. I wanted to tell him how deeply I respected him, both as a man and an entertainer, but I knew Rodney would only think I was mocking him. Then, one night, I got the most frightening phone call of my life.

Rodney had begun to feel that perhaps it was his fault that he never received any respect, and, disconsolate, he decided to end it all. He told me over the phone that in a fit of despair he had swallowed a bottle of sleeping pills.

"Rodney," I screamed into the phone, "please, listen, you must get to a doctor!"

"I just left his office, Norm. He told me to have a few drinks, try to get some sleep."

I didn't want to tell Rodney, but I thought that was one of the most disrespectful things I'd ever heard a doctor suggest. But Rodney already knew all too well. When he was away from the spotlight and alone with me, he would tell me his secret truth, all summed up in one sad sentence: "I tell you, Norm, it's the story of my life; I don't get no respect."

And so it went with Rodney Dangerfield. It reminded me of that line in the Scriptures: "What doth it profit a man if he gains the whole world but don't get no respect, no respect at all? Are you kidding me?"

I was also pretty down during this time. I felt I'd had my big chance on *Star Search* and blown it. In my dreams I often saw the angry eyes of Ed McMahon. But one fateful night, while watching *The Tonight Show Starring Johnny Carson,* everything at once became diamond clear to me. My melancholia lifted and I was overcome with joy and hope. What did I care about Ed McMahon? The world didn't revolve around Ed McMahon. The world revolved around the man sitting to his immediate left every night at eleven-thirty: the King and the Kingmaker, Johnny Carson. I knew I had to get on *The Tonight Show.* And I knew, in that moment, that I would. I knew deep in my soul that Johnny would make me an overnight star, and that it would happen very soon. I drank a handle of bourbon that night, alone and in glory.

Late in the fall of 1991, things were different for comedians. Johnny Carson could make your career with a wave of his hand. Here's how it worked: You went out there, you did your six minutes, and if Johnny liked you enough he'd wave his arm, inviting you to join him at his desk, and you'd sit beside him and he would anoint you and you would become a star. No other man could do that. Problem was, Carson had already announced his retirement and my time was running out on being anointed. But every time I went onstage in Los Angeles, my chance of getting on *Carson* increased, and I was doing as many sets as possible.

It was near Christmas when I came offstage at The World Famous Comedy Store and was approached by a small, unassuming man. You can spot a bigshot in Hollywood because he wears a pin-stripe suit and chews on a fat cigar. He's never unassuming. He's always assuming as hell.

"Hi, my name's Jim McCauley, and I'm the talent booker for *The Tonight Show*," the man said. Hollywood is a town filled with fakes and phonies. Charlatans and mountebanks, just waiting to take advantage of a country hick like me. I quickly deduced that this Jim McCauley character was about as authentic as a pound of pimento loaf. So I decided two could play that game.

"Is that so? Well, it's sure nice to meet you, Jim. My name's Norm Macdonald and I'm the King of Spain."

The man chuckled nervously. He knew I was onto him but he continued nonetheless. "As you know, Johnny is retiring in May, and he'd really like to break one last comic on the show. Norm, I think you're the guy."

"Well, that sounds fine to me, *Jim*. As a matter of fact it's been a dream of mine since I started stand-up. But, of course, I'll have to run it by my wife, the Queen of Spain. I'm sure you understand."

He laughed again but he couldn't give up the act. He was in it too deep. "Okay, then, we'll be in touch." He really slipped up there, because he had said "we" but he was all alone.

"Fair enough, I'll talk to you guys later," I said.

The next morning I got a call from a lady. "Mr. Macdonald, I have Jim McCauley for you."

"Sorry, never heard of him," I said, before hanging up.

The phone rang again. "Mr. Macdonald, I have Mr. McCauley, the man you met last night. The man who books comedians to appear on *The Tonight Show*."

"Oh, yes, of course, that Mr. McCauley. Yeah, put him on." I had to admire this guy's persistence.

"Hi, Norm, I think I found the perfect date. Second week of January we have Steve Martin and Elton John. I ran it past Johnny and he thinks it's great, because you'll be performing in front of him and Steve Martin and, fingers crossed, after your set you'll be sitting right between them."

Boy, had this guy done his homework. Steve Martin was my favorite comic, and I always considered Elton John to be a great singer as well as a hot piece of ass.

"Well, you see, the thing is this, Jim. January is not the perfect month, because that's when the people of Spain are at their most anti-monarchist. And if I was to leave the country at that point, there could be trouble in the streets. I don't know if you follow Spanish politics, Jim, but the queen is not well liked by her subjects. But what the hell. You only live once. I'll do it. I'll be on *The Tonight Show*."

"Congratulations, Norm. I think it's gonna be dynamite."

Well, a few weeks passed and I got a panicked call from my agent. "Norm, were you supposed to be on the Carson show tonight?"

"Don't tell me that guy is phoning YOU now."

"That guy is Jim McCauley and he books *The Tonight Show,* you idiot."

"I thought he was just a guy pulling a prank. Tell him I'll do it!"

"I already asked. He said you're dead in his eyes."

Boy, I really blew that one. Every comic's dream. I had it in my hand, and I'd let it sift through my fingers because I didn't know how to trust. I got very angry at myself and in a rage I returned to Madrid, where I took it out on my subjects by ruling them with an iron fist.

I first met Mr. Macdonald six months ago in the Random House offices here in the city. My publisher, Julie Grau, introduced us and informed me that he had a story that simply must be told. I'd heard this same speech from Julie many times before about many different people in that very office. There are so many stories that simply must be told. And it is my job to tell them.

Besides, as I said, I was a fan of his back in the nineties and was curious as to what had befallen the man. I had expected that Mr. Macdonald and I would hit it off that day.

Julie had motioned me into her office that afternoon while Mr. Macdonald was telling a story about how he hated Eskimos. It was not so much a story, really, as a string of words that was randomly assembled, incoherent, unending, and filled with hate. Every piece of clothing he wore advertised something he had done in the entertainment business at some time. He may as well have had "Has-been" stenciled on his forehead. I knew I had my work cut out for me with this one.

You wouldn't know it now, but I was a great man once. A fine young man, alive with ideas.

And suddenly I found myself an old man standing in a doorway as Mr. Macdonald spoke of how he didn't trust Eskimos and never would. I had never felt such instant animus toward anyone. And I remember thinking that this time I might not take the job. I might just walk out of the office.

But I stayed put as Mr. Macdonald mercifully finished his "story."

"... and so, anyways, the point is I've never met an Eskimo I liked.

Not once. Not ever. As a matter of fact I don't think I've ever even met an Eskimo. I call them blubber-eaters, by the way. And don't even get me started on the filthy Swedes." He struck the table with his fist and Julie burst into laughter. I'd heard many silly celebrities tell their silly stories in my time. They always amused me, the way a harmless child amuses me. But Mr. Macdonald appalled me. The way a harmful child appalls me.

For the first time, he fixed his sluggard's eyes on me. "Who are you, old man?"

"The name's Keane, Mr. Macdonald. Terence Keane." I extended my hand and he shook it with great strength, the way weak men always do. He finally stopped and I stood there, clasping and unclasping my hand, hoping the brute hadn't broken it in his effort to prove his manhood. "I will be your ghostwriter."

Mr. Macdonald lit up a cigarette in a nonsmoking building and shot a look at Julie. Julie, abashed, cast her eyes down.

"Oh, yes, Terence, Norm was just explaining to me that he has no need for a ghostwriter, only a secretary."

"That's right, mister," said Mr. Macdonald. "I'm a great writer. Written sketches, jokes, gags, all kinds of things. A memoir will be nothing for a guy like me. Problem is, I never learned to type. Back when I went to school, very few boys took any typing classes, if you catch my drift. What about you, Keane, did you ever take typing classes?"

He looked at me with a stupid smirk. Of course I'd caught his drift. It was the kind of drift you catch upon entering a gas station restroom. But I wasn't about to be cowed by this bullying clown.

"As a matter of fact I did, yes. Most useful class I took in high school. I can type seventy-five words a minute."

Macdonald looked over at Julie.

"I guess he'll do. Although I gotta tell you, when I pictured having a secretary, I figured she'd have a nice set of cans." Then he looked at me. "No offense, Keane, but yours look kinda floppy."

And then he let out a big hoary laugh, which was followed by

Julie's delighted squeal. "Oh, you are incorrigible, Norm, absolutely incorrigible. Isn't he, Terence?"

"Yes," I managed, "a true scapegrace."

I just stood there, burning up inside, and I guess Julie noticed, because she stopped laughing and turned to me.

"Of course, Terence, the deal would be the same as if you were the ghostwriter. The standard ten percent plus. Mr. Macdonald will receive a million upon receipt of the manuscript, and you will be paid a hundred thousand."

That cooled me down considerably, because that was a great deal of money for a celebrity memoir, especially a celebrity who hadn't worked in years.

"Wow," Mr. Macdonald said, "100K? That's easy money for you, Keane. I'll tell you the stories and all you have to do is write them down, word for word. That's it. You don't have to add your own opinions. Nobody's interested. If you can type as fast as you claim, we should be able to finish this thing in a week."

I looked at him closely to see if he was joking. He wasn't.

"I'll tell you what, Mr. Macdonald, why don't I begin with a little cursory research on you and we can get to work presently. I feel this collaboration will work out splendidly, sir. Just splendidly. How does that sound to you?"

"It sounds womanish."

"I beg your pardon."

"I mean the way you say 'splendidly.' Just sounds womanish, that's all. Now, don't get me wrong. I don't care what filthy things a man does with another man when they lay down together, but I just don't want any words like 'splendidly' showing up in this book. You understand me, brother?"

His eyes were dull and he took a menacing step toward me, and I backed up to the door. And in a moment I was out on the streets of the big busy city and away from the vile man and it felt fine. As a matter of fact, it felt splendid. Splendid. Splendid. Splendidly. Splendidly. Splendidly. Splendidly. Splendidly. Splendidly. SPLENDIDLY. SPLENDIDLY.

SPLENDIDLY. SPLENDIDLY.

14

LIVE FROM NEW YORK

"Oh, now I understand," says Adam Eget. "Of course. Everything happens for a reason. And the reason you did really bad at *Star Search* was so that you could not get *The Tonight Show*. Of course. It's so clear now."

"Adam Eget, are you trying to be sarcastic?"

His eyes lower. "I suppose."

"There's more to the story," Gabe says. "But I'm not gonna be around to listen to it again. I hear there's a juicy thirty–sixty game over at the Bellagio. See you later. Be careful out there."

And just like that, Gabe is gone. "Tell me the rest of the story, Norm."

"Sure," I say. "I'll tell you and one other guy. See, I'm writing a book and they gave me a secretary, and, get this, the secretary is a man!"

"Is this one of those riddles?" Adam Eget says. "I'm not good at those."

"No riddle, no joke. He's a man-secretary. He can even type. I phone and tell him stories and he types them out. I met him before this trip and I moved in with him for a month. I figured that would be way more than enough time to finish the book, but I guess the old fool couldn't type as fast as he'd claimed."

"Does the man-secretary have a nice house, Norm?"

"It's okay. I was gonna go back there and finish the book, but then I got the plan."

Adam Eget puts a big smile on his squid face. "Say, Norm, why don't you go back to the man-secretary and live with him till you're finished?"

"Nice try," I say, and I phone Keane's number and get his answering machine. That makes me happy. If he answered, he'd be sure to talk, and that would just slow me down. "Okay, Keane. Okay, Adam Eget. Listen, and hear about my first week at *SNL*." That was a long time ago, so I take a deep, deep drag and hold the magic stuff in my lungs, although it fights to get out. Finally, I can't take it anymore and I lean over and cough like hell. When I look up again, there it is. The past. It's directly in my face, like a forgotten child who's hunted me down to find out when I'll be returning with that pack of cigarettes.

After the *Carson* episode, my agent fired me and I got laughed out of Hollywood. I ended up in New York, where I slept in the Central Park Zoo, next to the polar bears. I got lucky—Robert Morton, the booker for *Late Night with David Letterman*, was at my first show at Catch a Rising Star. The next day I got a call that would change my life.

"You're on the show. Just one question: You're not that idiot who turned down *Carson*, right?"

"No," I said. I had my suspicions about him, but I had learned my lesson about trust, and it turned out that Morty was the real deal. A month later, David Letterman, the funniest man in the world, put me on his show and gave me his stamp of approval.

Everything moved quickly after that. Adam Sandler had been a friend since my early days of stand-up and had always had my back. It was Adam who persuaded Jim Downey, the head writer of *SNL*, to watch my *Letterman* performance. "He's not that idiot who turned down *Carson*?" said Jim.

"Yes," said Adam.

Jim laughed. "Oh, we've gotta get that guy on the show." Jim, in turn, recommended me to Lorne Michaels. "He's not that idiot who turned down *Carson*?" said Lorne.

"No," said Jim.

People were beginning to talk about me, and that's always good news. As Adolf Hitler once said, all publicity is good publicity.

Soon after, I was offered the opportunity to audition for Lorne.

Back when I started, Lorne began the year by taking all the cast and crew to a place called Mohonk, a lakeside resort at the foot of the Catskills. The idea was that the new writers and performers could meet and bond with the veterans in a relaxed atmosphere.

We were like one great big dysfunctional family, except we were not related and we all got along famously. But we were great, and we were big. The year I started, Jay Mohr and Sarah Silverman also joined the cast, and Dave Attell became one of the writers. They were all very cool and very talented, and this made me very afraid.

I was not used to seeing famous people, so the week at Mohonk was both intimidating and exciting. The stars like Mike Myers, Phil Hartman, and Tim Meadows were all there, along with legendary writers Robert Smigel, Ian Maxtone-Graham, Tom Davis, and Jim Downey. I instantly bonded with Downey, who was the only person at *SNL* who had completed less formal education than I had, having dropped out of school in the second grade. But Downey had street smarts, and even if he couldn't tell you who Newton or Shakespeare was, he could tell you plenty about the guys he had met in the streets. Like this one guy named Bill. And this other guy named Bob.

The first night at Mohonk, the whole cast and crew gathered in the dining room. Adam Sandler, David Spade, Rob Schneider, and I were sitting at a table together, and they were going on and on about how funny Chris Farley was and how much I was going to love him, but I'd heard that about plenty of guys in my time. I'd be the judge of that. The dinner was winding down with a lot of boring comedy talk about what was funny and what wasn't funny when, suddenly, something funny happened. The doors burst open and a naked Farley entered, doing his impression of a salad—shoving baby tomatoes up his ass and dousing himself with oil and vinegar. The room went crazy and Sandler yelled in my ear, "What did I tell you!?" They were right: I'd never seen anything close to that before.

Later in the evening, when I was officially introduced to Chris, I was surprised to find he'd taken on a serious tone. He leaned in to me and whispered that there was something very important he had to tell me, and it was a matter of some urgency. He secreted me to a room where we could be alone, locked the door, and cased the place, to be sure no one was listening. He made me swear that what he was about to tell me must never leave the room. I was thrilled that the great Farley was taking me, a complete stranger, into his confidence and excited to learn what all this cloak-and-dagger was about.

After I took the oath of secrecy, Chris drew me close and whispered in my ear.

"Pat is actually a WOMAN!!!!!!!!!"

And then that big Chris laugh. Man, I miss that laugh. That big Chris laugh.

During that trip, I talked deep into the night with Lorne Michaels. He explained to me that it was a time of profound change at *SNL*. The brilliant sketch players—Dana Carvey, Jon Lovitz, Jan Hooks, along with the tack-sharp Dennis Miller—had all ended their tenure on the show. Mike Myers and Phil Hartman would soon be following suit. It was hard to imagine they could be replaced. Who would dare fill the shoes of the greatest sketch troupe ever assembled?

Those who came after were cut from wholly different cloth, Lorne explained. There were four: Farley, Schneider, Spade, and the top dog, Sandler. Other than Farley, none of these boys had any experience in sketch acting. They didn't come from Second City or the Groundlings; they came from the smoky nightclubs of America. They were stand-ups and they worked alone. It looked bad for the new cast, and Lorne predicted that the press would mention it often.

Lorne called them "The Not Ready for the Not Ready for Prime Time Players." But the boys were adapting, Lorne explained. They were using their stand-up skills to their advantage, playing not to each other or the studio audience but over all that and to the camera, to the home audience itself. They performed in the sketch and watched it at the same time, often laughing at the silliness of it all.

"These kids are in the serious business of deconstruction, and in Sandler's case, it will often rise to a glorious dereliction of duty."

Most all of this I didn't understand, but I nodded whenever I felt it was appropriate and I certainly agreed with Lorne that these four guys were the Beatles of Comedy.

Lorne told me that this change in the show's tone would not sit well with many of the writers, and I soon learned what he meant. There was a sharp divide between the ones who embraced the new comedians and the ones who rejected them.

Lorne Michaels, Tim Herlihy, Ian Maxtone-Graham, Jim Downey, and Robert Smigel loved the anarchy of it all. But others vocally did not. And that week at Mohonk was filled with dissension between the two camps.

On the final night, Adam Sandler told me the following season would be a rough, divisive one, and he wanted to know which side I'd take. I told him I wanted to be on the side of the guy who had shoved the baby tomatoes up his ass.

Adam smiled.

15

A LITTLE FAME

"That's when you moved to Regency House, right, Norm?"

"Yes. That's right, Adam Eget, remember the Regency House?" Makes me kinda sad remembering.

They say my Father's house has many mansions, but the one I live in now is no great digs. Four men to a room, and you have to be back before nine in the evening and you can't have whiskey on your breath or Mrs. Sullivan will turn her back to you, and the hard pavement of the Nickel will be your pillow. But back in the day. Oh, back in the day. The Regency House.

The Regency House sat on Central Park West and had a lot of kids from *SNL* living in it. Kevin Nealon, Phil Hartman, Timmy Meadows, even the great Adam Sandler, and Lori Jo Hoekstra. Lori Jo was a writer's assistant who got me into the joint. It was great to move out of the Central Park Zoo. Polar bears make terrible neighbors.

Lori Jo was the smartest and funniest woman I had ever met, and she was hotter than a two-dollar pistol to boot. She eventually became my producer on Weekend Update and then my producing partner on everything thereafter. Truth be told, any success I ever attained would have been impossible without Lori Jo.

I lived way up on the thirty-fifth floor of the Regency House and had a beautiful view of the wall of another thirty-fifth floor of another New York apartment building. We were a stone's throw away from work and I'd often walk there with Sandler, who everyone knew and loved. The doorman, Steve, always had a good word for Adam and liked to talk to him about the show from the week before. Sometimes he liked it and sometimes he didn't, but he always loved Adam. Adam introduced me to Steve and told him that I was on the show as well. Steve looked puzzled and I explained that, although I was technically on the show, I had yet to actually be on the TV. Steve looked even more puzzled. "Don't worry, Steve," Sandler said. "You'll be seeing plenty of Normie." That's all it took. After that I was good with Steve.

One day I left my apartment and got on the elevator. There was a girl standing in it. Her head was bent down and she quietly wept, so I ignored her. On the twenty-first floor a man got on the elevator. He was a real gregarious New York kinda guy. As soon as he saw the girl, he jumped into action.

"Hey, honey, what's the matter?" he asked, and she mumbled something through sniffles, to which he replied, "Lemme tell you something: Everything's gonna turn out all right, okay? This guy knows." And he motioned to me, but I didn't know, so I stayed silent. We all got out of the elevator and I went to get my mail, and when I got back to the lobby the gregarious fellow was still talking to the girl, who was still quietly weeping. He was telling her how things always worked out, how matters that were substantial today were trivial tomorrow. He told her that he would take her to have coffee in the Greek diner around the corner and that everything was gonna be just fine, and she nodded as they left.

On my way back up to my apartment, I was spotted by Steve the doorman. His eyes were bright and he smiled. I knew why. He had seen me on the show the previous Saturday. It was my first time on-screen. Tim Herlihy had put me in a *Star Trek* sketch, where I had one line: "Beam me up, Scotty." That was good enough for Steve the doorman.

"Hey, hey, look who it is. Beam Me Up Scotty!!!! How are you feeling this fine morning, Beam Me Up Scotty?"

"I'm good, Steve, really good. I'm going to go upstairs to my apartment, have a cigarette and coffee, and read the *Daily News*."

"Atta boy, Beam Me Up Scotty," said Steve the doorman.

From then on, that was how Steve the doorman knew me. When I got home from work I could rely on a hearty "Good evening to you, Beam Me Up Scotty." He was always excited to see me, because I was a famous guy who went on the TV every Saturday night and said, "Beam me up, Scotty." The problem was, only he and I knew that, and everyone in the vicinity would just look at me odd. One time I was going through the door and Steve was having a conversation with a friend, which he abruptly stopped when he saw that such a famous figure as I was at the door.

"Hey, Beam Me Up Scotty, I'd like you to meet a friend of mine, John; he's a good guy, always been there for me, you know what I mean. You don't find that often in this life. John, I'd like you to meet Beam Me Up Scotty."

John shook my hand and said, "Sorry, what was your name?"

Steve got embarrassed that his friend was so ignorant of popular culture, and he slapped the back of his glove on the chest of John's heavy coat and reproached him. "What's the matter with you, Johnny? This is Beam Me Up Scotty, from the TV." Then he looked at me. "Go ahead. Do it for him."

"Beam me up, Scotty," I said.

John just looked at me for a long moment, bewildered, then said, "Oh, yeah, sure. I know you."

"Sure you know him," Steve said. "He's Beam Me Up Scotty."

And outside the Regency House, we all laughed loudly for different reasons in the cold autumn of New York.

A little fame can be an embarrassing thing, and I was to learn that lesson often. I mean, I'm used to it now, like when Mr. Abernathy says, "Hey, Piscopo, that stew's not all for you, ya know." Mr. Abernathy, he's lived at the boardinghouse forever, and when I first moved in, he called me Piscopo and I never corrected him. I should have years ago, but if you don't do something right away, you never do it. And, after all, one name is as good as another.

One time, that first year on *SNL,* I got recognized by an actual celebrity. It was Slash, whom I had admired for some time both for his incredible guitar playing and his hat. It would never occur to me that a guy like Slash would even know a bum like me existed. But that's the great thing about showbiz. A famous guy like Slash, whom you've never met in your life, runs up to you in the streets of New York, shakes your hand, and treats you like you're both old friends.

"How you doing, buddy? What's new?"

"Oh, not much, Slash, just same-old same-old. You know how it is. Hurry up and wait."

"Yeah, don't I know it."

When you're in showbiz and you meet another guy in showbiz, you're supposed to play it cool, but me, I get real nervous. Slash asked if we could speak in confidence, and so we found a corner where we could talk and be unheard by the unfamous.

Slash leaned in to me close.

"Have you talked to Chucky lately?"

I didn't know anyone named Chucky. "Not for a while, no," I said. "Why?"

Slash got even quieter. "He's not in good shape. When was the last time you talked to him?"

I felt sweat everywhere. "I don't know. Probably four months. He seemed pretty good, considering."

I knew I had to get out of there quickly, before Slash realized I was not who I was pretending to be, a close friend of his who shared a mutual friend named Chucky with him. Chucky, who was not in good shape. But I could hardly just run away.

"Listen," said Slash, "if you have a chance and could go see him, it'd mean the world to him. Like I said, he's not in good shape. Although, I guess, knowing Chucky, that shouldn't come as a big surprise."

"No," I said meaningfully, "it sure shouldn't," and then I shook my head sadly, and so did Slash.

I still think of Chucky from time to time. I like to hope Chucky's doing better, but knowing Chucky as I do by pretending to know Chucky, chances aren't good.

Oh, and that girl who was quietly sobbing on the elevator— I saw her again, but only once, and it was the damnedest thing. It was months later, and I entered the elevator and there she was. Except this time she wasn't alone. She was with the gregarious guy, the guy I'd seen console her months earlier, but now he wasn't consoling her, he was yelling at her and telling her she had no business looking through his drawers. Her head was bent down and she quietly wept.

Years ago, I was friends with Andy Warhol and was present when he uttered his prophetic statement, "In the future, everybody will be famous for fifteen minutes." Andy did not live to see his words take shape in our world.

I work in the following manner. I listen to my subject, and I absorb all he has to say. When I discover his essence, I become him. My process is the same that Lee Strasberg teaches actors; you could call it method writing, I suppose.

I had Mr. Macdonald over to my brownstone for an afternoon tea and he stayed a month. It was the longest month of my life as I listened to what he called his "great antidotes." These were either dishwater-dull true stories or preposterous lies—he wrote The Jerk for Steve Martin, he was Canada's minister of defense, he used to like brussels sprouts, but not anymore. I'm still afraid to enter my guest room, which is filled knee-high with his SNL jackets, Norm Show T-shirts, and Dirty Work hats. And, hiding among his laundry, hypodermic needles. Now he phones me and I leave the poor answering machine to listen.

But, still, I remain confident that I will find the truth of the man, which will then enable me to become him. I am determined to make Mr. Macdonald appear interesting, engaging, and, most of all, funny. This last bit is the most difficult task, because the man is simply not funny. Fortunately I have a razor-sharp sense of humor, always have. Here's an example of what I find humorous:

A professor of history buys a dog, and a colleague asks, "Have you thought of a name for the beast?"

"Why, certainly," says the professor. "I was thinking of naming it the Holy Roman Empire."

"But why?" asks his bewildered friend.

"Well, it's really quite simple," replies the history professor. "You see, the dog is neither holy, nor Roman, nor an empire."

I should say I recounted this joke to Mr. Macdonald at an early meeting and was answered with the blankest of stares. Pearls before swine.

But my opinions are meaningless, because in this upside-down world, Mr. Macdonald is famous and I am not.

In the future, everyone will be anonymous for fifteen minutes.

16

WINNING BIG

've been winning a lot of money very quickly. Gabe and I are sitting in the coffee shop, looking at his iPad, which is displaying properties in Billings. Things are moving beautifully fast. Can it really keep up?

My bets are consistent, between ten and twenty thousand per game, usually one game a night, on a rare occasion two. Much to the delight and surprise of Gabe, I have had five straight nights where I've made no bets at all. But Gabe is not the only one noticing. Jimmy, Bill, and Jake, who all work at the Mirage Sports Book and are fine fellows, have noticed my restraint, and I can tell from their faces that they are not happy. It isn't the money. They've seen me win much more in much less time. I've never made them break sweat. But this time I haven't been playing like a loser, and the boys at the Book don't like this one bit. Where is the old Norm, sweating, pacing, wincing, losing? Who is this reasonable man making these reasonable bets? Gabe and I agree that tomorrow I will pay off my Mirage marker, take my profit, and move my action over to Caesars Palace. But I have one last bet to make before we go.

An hour later I'm in line at the Sports Book.

I have been up all night studying the lines, and I've discovered a trend that I don't think any of the big boys have seen. This is when you can make serious money. My plan is to bet higher than my regular bet, since Texas looks like a lock. I decide to bet thirty thousand dollars on the underdog Rangers, which would net me 75K and change. But I never make that bet. I never make that bet because Providence steps in at the last second.

"Ten million dollars on Fernandez," a man whispers.

"Certainly, Mr. Guardino," another man whispers.

In the line next to mine stands a hulking man whose expensive suit makes him look no less a brute. He reaches the front just as I do and opens a suitcase filled with chips, which the teller begins to painstakingly count. I look up at the board to see who this mafioso is betting on. Fernandez is a boxer, and he pays 11 to 1. This guy is betting ten million dollars on a huge underdog. That's good enough for me. I empty my pockets.

"Three hundred sixty thousand on Fernandez," I say.

Jimmy looks at me suspiciously. "I'm gonna need authorization for that," he says, and he makes a call to the back office. Moments later, the head of the Sports Book, Jake, comes out. "You sure you want to bet this much, Norm?" He knows if I win, it will pay four million. He also knows I have been winning consistently for a week. What he does not know is that once I win this bet I will never make another wager as long as I live. He thinks a good long time before finally rapping the top of the table. "Okay, book it. Good luck."

The fight isn't on for another four hours, so I wander over to the poker room and sweat Gabe for a bit. I decide I'll give him the business. "I bet it all, Gabe. I had a hunch." I want to get a rise out of him.

"Oh, God, this would never have happened if the chips were in the safe where they should be. What's the bet?"

"It's a boxer. His name's Fernandez."

A guy from the other side of the table hears me and lets out a big laugh. "Fernandez? That bum has a glass jaw. He won't last thirty seconds."

Gabe checks his iPhone. "He's even money."

"Yeah," I say. "He is now. The line tends to move dramatically when a guy from the mob bets ten million dollars."

"You're kidding," says Gabe. "You saw this?"

"Yeah, that's why I got my bet in at eleven to one while they were still counting his ton of chips."

Gabe smiles. "Lucky man."

"Thanks, Gabe."

That evening I invite everyone I meet in the casino to my room, and we settle around the giant TV screen. We have shrimp cocktail and beef on skewers and bowls of ice cream and tumblers of scotch and cigars and women and just about everything a man could want. In my hand is a ticket that will soon be worth four million dollars, much more than my goal. I get my realtor from Billings on the phone and we talk for a good hour. I explain I'll be needing a bigger ranch. And I explain I will be needing an arsenal of weapons to keep the bad people away from the ranch. After I get off the phone, I conference with Adam Eget in the corner to explain in detail what his duties will be on the ranch. Before I can finish, the fighters enter the ring. The man announces the challenger Fernandez's name and my hotel room goes nuts. The ref is giving his instructions to the fighters, and I notice how calm Fernandez is as he stares his opponent down. We all rise to our feet as the bell sounds to begin round one.

Fernandez moves in quickly, and the other fellow hits him and knocks him out.

The hotel room is silent for a moment. Then I scream as loud as

I can. I grab a pillow from the sofa and rip it open, sending feathers flying. I hit the wall as hard as I can, and there is a huge hole where my now-broken hand was. I grab the glass table in the center of the room and overturn it, sending shrimp and ice and nachos and drinks spilling onto the carpet. I run over to the counter where the liquor and glasses are and, with a backward swipe of my arm, I clear it, and broken glass flies everywhere. My guests shield their eyes and try to find the door. There is a great deal of noise now as people stampede out of the room. Now it is only me and Adam Eget, who is sitting on the edge of the sofa.

"What's the problem, buddy?" he says.

I kick him as hard as I can in the shins and race down to the Sports Book. "What the hell happened?" I shout to no one and everyone.

Jimmy smiles his wry smile. "An eleven-to-one dog lost. It's been known to happen, Norm."

"But, Jimmy, what about that mob guy? He bet ten million."

Jimmy laughs. "Oh my God, Norm, why didn't you ask me? That was no mob guy. That was Longshot Louie. He bets anything that's five to one or better. He's got so much money he doesn't care."

"Longshot Louie?" I said. "Longshot Louie?"

"Yeah," says Jimmy, in his calm, seen-it-all voice. "Speaking of long shots, you been watching the ball game? Nobody saw that coming."

In a daze, I look up at a TV screen and see that the Texas Rangers are ahead 5–1 in the ninth.

I get the boys and we check out to go over to Caesars, and I'm seething. Gabe keeps saying, "Man on tilt." We finally get there, go through the whole procedure again, and get three hundred thousand dollars in chips. This time I make fifteen bets on baseball games, for twenty thousand a game. Hours later I'm lying on my new bed, hugging my new pillow. Adam Eget sits in a chair beside the bed, sweating hard and staring at me. Gabe enters.

"Hey, pal, I heard you been flipping coins. What's the damage?"

That's what Gabe calls it when you make a bet that is 50–50 except for the juice. He calls it flipping coins against a really lucky guy.

Adam Eget jumps to his feet. "Gabe, he lost fifteen straight bets. What are the odds of that, right?" I wish he hadn't asked, because I know Gabe will know the answer.

"About one in thirty thousand," he says, and this gets Adam Eget excited and more sweat drips down his big squidbilly head.

"Then he's due, right, Gabe? He's due. I mean, what's the chance of him losing another?"

"A little more than fifty percent."

"But that makes no sense. He's due."

"Don't tell me. Tell the coin."

I tell them both to scram and I lie there, wallowing in my man-made pride and cursing all that is good in the world. I pick up the phone. "You guys got any Wild Turkey 101 down there?"

"Yes, sir."

"Send up all you got."

Five weeks pass.

17

FIRST WEEK AT WORK

The languorous joy of Mohonk, where we had had breakfast on cedar tables in the morning and spent our evenings laughing with drink and new friendships in front of a roaring bonfire next to the lake, became, as all things do, a memory. The next week we were on the seventeenth floor of Rockefeller Center, a beehive of activity and stinging rejection, where we had to learn and learn fast.

We were all just kids back then. Well, not kids, really, but we were very, very immature. I got to know my fellow freshmen very quickly: Jay Mohr, Dave Attell, and Sarah Silverman. One of them I loved and one of them I hated.

I hated Dave Attell. But I only hated him because I loved Sarah Silverman, and she loved Dave Attell.

The first year was tough. Sarah, Jay, and I had been hired as featured players. It was a tough position to be in—languishing somewhere just shy of being a full writer and a full performer. We were expected to write sketches for the big dogs, but we were also allowed to write ourselves small parts in the sketches. The problem was, we were stand-up comics and we were competing with actual sketch writers, who knew what they were doing. These writers were very smart and literate, and many of them had attended Ivy League schools. The roster was made up of Ian Maxtone-Graham, Lew Morton, Dave Mandel, Steve Koren, Marilyn Suzanne Miller, Steve Lookner, and—the brightest and funniest of them all—Jim Downey. You just didn't get much smarter than these young lions of comedy. That's why I was so flattered when I learned that they had given me the nickname "Einstein."

"Hey, nice sketch this week, Einstein."

"I bet you have some good ideas for Alec Baldwin, huh, Einstein?"

"Hey, Einstein, we're hungry. Can you go get us a buncha sandwiches, Einstein?"

That kinda thing.

I was honored that these smart, educated folk had given me the moniker. But the truth was, I was nowhere near as smart as Alfred Einstein. Shoot, I wasn't even as smart as that new scientist, the one with the wheelchair and the funny way of talking. But I wasn't gonna let the eggheads and bluestockings in the writers' room know that.

Despite the high praise of my co-workers, I had trouble getting any of my sketches on the air. But I remembered what Downey had said and stayed close to the Fab Four and their leader, my friend Adam Sandler. Some of the writers would give me bit parts in skits, which allowed me to keep my job. Ian Maxtone-Graham, Adam McKay, Steve Higgins, and Tim Herlihy were especially kind, and Sandler was always sure to throw me a bone.

One time I came close to blowing it with Sandler, because I was a rookie and not used to the nuances of acting in sketches.

Probably the toughest part of acting, and something you never learn in stand-up, is having the sharp wit to react when someone calls you by a different name. Sandler had written me into a sketch as his co-star. It was a huge opportunity for me, and I was determined not to blow it like I had blown every other opportunity in the joke I called my life. I studied that sketch from front to back, which I had been told by Downey was the correct order in which to study it. It was my big break, and I wasn't about to screw it up.

On Saturday night I was nervous but ready, like a great athlete. We were trying out the sketch at dress rehearsal. The only way you got the sketch on the real live show at 11:30 P.M. was to destroy at dress at 8:00 P.M.

Sandler hit me with his first line:

"Hey, Frank, did you hear about that meteor hurtling toward the earth?"

By this time, I lived in the same apartment building, the Regency House, that Adam lived in, and we shared an office, so I was good friends with him and he never called me Frank; he always called me Norm. Naturally, when he called me Frank I didn't respond, and so Adam repeated his line, but I noticed there was an edge in his voice. If I'd been thinking, I'd have realized at this point that I was Frank, because Adam and I were the only two people in the sketch, but I wasn't thinking. I was looking at things around the set, one table in particular. It was made of brown wood and reminded me of a table I'd once seen in a table store. So the two of us didn't say anything at all. About twenty minutes passed and finally the show ended. Boy, Adam was really steamed at me about that one. And Lorne was too.

Every Wednesday we would submit our sketches, and this is where the most curious thing would happen. From the beginning I had submitted my Answering Machine sketch, which I knew would be a blockbuster and in which I had a starring role. The sketch was based on the first joke I ever told onstage and was the funniest thing ever. Seriously. I wrote the sketch and brought it to table every single week. Some weeks it would get no laughs at all. Others it would get two, or three, or four. That's the way comedy works. They either hate you or they don't completely hate you. You can never tell which it will be beforehand.

Every time I submitted the Answering Machine sketch, I would be sure to write Sarah Silverman in, as she was struggling, like me, and any airtime was valuable to her. Also, using Sarah gave me a dynamite end to the sketch.

Sarah would say, "Boy, mister, these answering machines are really annoying." And I would say, "Frankly, lady, I don't give a damn," and then give Sarah a big smooch. This gave the sketch a big laugh at the end by spoofing a well-known motion picture, and it also allowed me to give a big smooch to Sarah, whom I was falling deeply in love with.

At the time, Sarah and Dave Attell ruled the New York stand-up scene. Sarah, with her sly, subversive satire masked by the sweetest of deliveries. And Attell, a joke machine to rival Dangerfield himself. She was elegant and unafraid. He was rumpled, unshaven, and a chain-smoker. They were the Bogey and Bacall of the New York comedy circle. What chance did I have? What woman was going to choose Alfred Einstein over Humphrey Bogart? Still, I vowed I would win Sarah's love.

No one at *SNL* knew more about matters of the heart than David Spade, so I asked his advice. "Just ask her out, buddy," Spade told me. Just ask her out. So simple and yet so incredibly complex. No wonder David Spade was so good with the ladies.

I was pulling an all-nighter in the writers' room, trying to finish the Answering Machine sketch for Wednesday's read-through, when I spotted Sarah in the hallway. I decided to make my intentions known. "You're dreadful pretty, Sarah," I said, "and I'd be honored if you would lay down with me. And not in the restroom either. I will take you out to a restaurant and you can order beefsteak that I will pay for. We will coo and whisper and smile meaningful smiles and we will reduce the whole world and its people to our small table and the two of us. And then, afterward, I will take you to my bed and we will be like swine."

She ran away, and I realized that I'd made a big mistake. You see, Sarah was a liberated woman and she didn't need any man to buy her beefsteak. She made exactly the same salary as I did, minus the thirty percent that they automatically took off on account of she was a woman. And what a woman! In a way Sarah's lucky she never met the payroll clerk at *SNL,* or they might have taken off sixty percent.

The day after my clumsy pass I was served a restraining order that said I was not allowed to be within one hundred yards of my loved one. This made the cameramen on the show furious, because when Sarah and I were in the same sketch, they had to resort to ridiculously wide shots. I fell into a deep depression, heartbroken.

About a week later I walked into the Comedy Cellar to do a set. I had some new material and wanted to try it out (they had recently come out with a new telephone that had its own built-in answering machine), and the first thing I saw was the two of them, Dave and Sarah, canoodling at a corner table. They may as well have been up in a tree K-I-S-S-I-N-G. Well, I saw red and I went over to Colin Quinn. Colin was and is the smartest comedian alive and a great guy to boot. (This was long before he joined the cast of *SNL* and destroyed my life.)

"Colin," I said, "you're from New York. Where does a guy go to hire a hit man?"

Colin laughed. "What do you want with a hit man?"

"Can you keep a secret, Colin? I plan to have Dave Attell murdered and then, once he's out of the way, convince Sarah to lay down with me."

I should have paused to give Colin a chance to answer my question regarding his ability to keep a secret before I spilled my whole plan. As it turned out, Colin Quinn was a huge blabbermouth, who wound up prating like a magpie about the entire murder plot as soon as he got the chance. But I didn't know that then.

"Don't worry," I said. "There's between fifty and seventy-five dollars in it for you."

"Are you completely serious about this, Norm? I mean, there's plenty of fish in the sea."

I knew right away he wasn't talking about fish. Colin was the king of metaphors. He meant there were plenty of ladies in the sea.

"No offense, Colin, but the longer it takes for me to listen to your yapping, the longer it will take to have Dave Attell murdered and that very night lay down with Sarah."

Colin looked very nervous but finally said, "All right. I know a guy."

Colin called me the next day and said it was all set up. I was to meet the hit man at the corner booth of the Stage Deli the next day at noon. I asked Colin if he could change it to the Carnegie Deli, because it is a far superior deli. He said it was too late so I thanked him, but he had to have heard the bitter disappointment in my voice. I mean, if you're going to meet a hit man at a Midtown deli, why the Stage Deli? Why not the Carnegie Deli?

The next day, I sat in the Stage Deli and waited for the hit man to arrive. He was late, so I spent my time thinking about the delicious pastrami on rye they had at the Carnegie Deli and how I would not be eating one today. I saw a police officer enter the joint and I got nervous. When he slipped into the booth across from me, I got really nervous.

"You Norm?" he asked.

"I'm not talking to any coppers," I said.

"Who's a copper?" the cop asked.

"You are."

"I'm no copper. Where did you get a ridiculous idea like that?"

"You're wearing a police uniform." I was very good at spotting cops.

He looked down at himself and saw that I was right and began sweating profusely and stuttering and hitting his forehead twice with the palm of his hand and saying, "STUPID! STUPID!"

It took him a few minutes to compose himself, but finally he said, "Oh, this. You see, I've been walking the beat the last ten years and I just got promoted to undercover cop. But you know what they say. Old habits die hard."

He seemed relaxed again.

"So you're an undercover cop," I said. "Why should I talk to you?"

Well, he started the whole sweating and stuttering and hitting-his-forehead routine all over again. I'd just got up to leave when he blurted out, "I'm a bad cop. A dirty cop."

"You are?"

"Of course I am. That's what makes me such a good hit man. I have my own gun, and nobody ever suspects a cop."

The waitress came up and addressed the hit man with the police costume on. "Sir, I'm going to have to ask you to keep your voice down. You're frightening many of the customers."

The hit man had been speaking very loudly, in a sort of a panic. I would find out later that he wasn't a bad cop at all. I mean, he was a bad cop in the sense that he was no good at being a cop, but he was not a corrupt cop.

He pulled out a large tape recorder and hit the play button and the record button simultaneously and we began hammering out a deal. He would murder Dave Attell and in return I would give him $355. We haggled for well over an hour before finally settling on the $355 figure, which made me very angry after he arrested me and I realized he could have just accepted my first offer and saved us both a lot of time. When I got to the precinct they told me I was allowed one phone call.

"Hello, Colin, it's Norm. You're from New York. Where does a guy go to hire an attorney?"

18

THE TRIAL

Only a month earlier I had been on national television, appearing in bit parts in Ellen Cleghorne sketches. And now here I stood before a judge, wearing some sort of ridiculous orange jumpsuit, found guilty by a jury of my peers, about to be sentenced, and trying to figure how it had come to this. And maybe I was guilty, but of what, really? Attempting to hire a hit man to kill a close friend of mine? Well, if they convicted everybody who was guilty of that, they'd have to build a lot more prisons in this country, brother.

And what had I done anyway? I had never actually met a hit man. By the prosecution's own admission, the police officer I met with at the Stage Deli had never killed a single man in exchange for cash. All I'd really done was eat a Reuben with a policeman. I had a very good lawyer and he tried to get the charge reduced to eating a Reuben with a policeman. But the judge didn't go for it.

I thought we had a pretty good defense. We made the point that people die every day; it's not such a big deal. We showed the jury a picture of Sarah Silverman and they all agreed she was a knockout, and one man even made a loud wolf whistle. We tried to get the jury to believe that I had an evil twin brother and it was he who was guilty and not me, and we even told them not to feel bad charging me with the crime because we understood that it was a natural mistake. But that fell apart when it turned out my evil twin brother had an ironclad alibi. He had been down south on a multistate killing spree at the time.

Even though I was found guilty, I never blamed my lawyer. I mean, he was no Ben Matlock, but he was good. The problem was, I was just too guilty. But I was a man, I'd made a mistake, and I was willing to face the consequences of my actions.

I started to think how maybe I should have taken that plea bargain, though. My lawyer was very good friends with the DA. He had come to me one day, giddy, and told me of the deal he had struck. If I pleaded guilty and apologized to Mr. Attell in court, I would receive a sentence of one midafternoon in prison.

"No way," I said. "I want my name cleared and I will never apologize to Dave Attell. He was the guy I was trying to have murdered. And you want ME to apologize to HIM?!!?" Well, now, as I stood to hear the judge's decision, that plea bargain was starting to look pretty good, and that sentence of one midafternoon was starting to seem pretty short.

"Mr. Macdonald, you are found guilty and sentenced to serve forty years in a maximum-security prison. Is there anything you would like to say to this court?"

Oh, I had plenty to say to this court, all right.

"Your Honor, you have sentenced me to prison, but let me say this. The real prisons in this country are the classrooms and the cubicles. The real prisons are the mausoleums we call houses, and the life sentence we are given is a job where we have to wear a tie that slowly strangles us and a woman who finds us full and leaves us empty. I will go to your prison; it is true. But there is something honest and true and noble about prison. You give up your freedom, yes.

But, in exchange, you are given a roof over your head, three squares a day, and all the morphine you want. And I guess that's good enough for the likes of me."

"There's no morphine in prison, son," the judge sighed.

"What??????"

I had clearly been misinformed.

19

DOING TIME

Prison was a scary place, and the first day was worst of all. The first thing that happened was the guards took away all of the stuff I'd brought from home. They took away my wallet and my keys and my forty pounds of Omaha Steaks and my cake with the file inside. They took away my *Dirty Work* hat and my *Norm Show* T-shirt and my *SNL* jacket and all the rest of my free-world clothes, and they made me wear their striped pajamas. They even took away my name, but that part was actually pretty cool because they gave me a number instead, like I was a robot from outer space. Mine was 6023102.

Then they walked me to my cell, past dangerous-looking convicts who chanted, "Fresh meat. Fresh meat. Fresh meat."

"You may as well stop with your chanting, boys," I answered. "I don't have a single Omaha Steak on me. They all got took." The convicts continued their chant, but there was a puzzled tone to it.

The guards threw me in a cell where a big sullen man was sitting on the lower of two steel bunks. He looked to be about three hundred pounds, without an ounce of fat on him. He had a square jaw and a dark forelock, which barely concealed a swastika tattoo.

"Hey, Rocco," said one of the guards as he tossed me to the cold gray floor, "we got some fresh meat for you."

"Don't you believe him, Rocco," I said. "They took all my fresh meat in the other room, and I wouldn't be surprised if they're gonna eat it themselves."

Rocco looked me over as the guards left.

"What are you in for?" he asked. I explained the whole situation with Sarah Silverman and Dave Attell and then I asked him the same. "Triple murder," he said.

I was shocked; any fool knows you can't murder a man more than once, and I told Rocco as much. He'd been railroaded on those last two counts, and I let him know I'd be more than happy to become his jailhouse lawyer and dedicate my life to gaining his freedom. After all, becoming a jailhouse lawyer had been a boyhood dream of mine, and here I was with an opportunity to make it come true! I knew logically that Rocco was completely innocent of at least two of the crimes he'd been convicted of. And I believed in my heart that he was most likely innocent of the other one too. After all, if a man is innocent of two murders, odds are he's innocent of the third. That's just grade-school arithmetic. I couldn't wait to get in front of that jury. I planned to go to the prison library first thing in the morning and start reading law books. And I'd had a little head start too. You see, I had seen every single episode of *Matlock* many times over.

"I'll set you free, Rocco. I promise you that."

Rocco started to get real excited at this news. He told me his first lawyers had convinced him to plead guilty. We both agreed that's the last thing anyone should ever do. We were on the same wavelength, and that's important when it comes to a lawyer and his client.

The first thing I suggested was that he lose the swastika tattoo. I didn't care, personally, about a man's politics, but if there's one thing

I'd learned from watching *Matlock,* it was this: Juries hate Hitler. Rocco claimed that he had just picked his tattoo out of a prison tattoo book. "Is there anything we can do?" he asked.

"Sure, I can just modify the tattoo—add some lines to it and easily make it into a tic-tac-toe board."

"That sounds good," said Rocco, but then he began to look troubled.

When I asked him what was wrong, Rocco said, "I was just wondering if the tic-tac-toe board is associated with another wicked man from history."

I smiled. "Do you consider Wink Martindale historically wicked?"

Rocco let out a roar of laughter. "Everyone loves Wink Martindale!" And for the first time I could see a glimmer of genuine hope.

The next day I went to the prison library to study, but I was disheartened when I found out that law books are long. Long books make me sleepy. A great lawyer must know his weaknesses and I knew almost all of mine. I decided that, instead of struggling through those books, I would rely on my vast knowledge of Ben Matlock's work. So Rocco and I began to practice courtroom scenarios in our small cell. I started by asking Rocco straight out if he was guilty of any of the three murders.

"Oh, I'm guilty all right, that's for sure. And the funny thing is, I have no remorse. I'd do it again tomorrow."

After hearing this, I made a key decision: Rocco would not be taking the stand. Our courtroom preparation had come to an end, and I felt ready to defend him before the judge.

The next day I changed Rocco's tattoo from a swastika to a tic-tac-toe board. And while I was at it, I went one step further. Using Rocco's wide, heavily muscled back as my canvas, I used my needle and green ink to fashion a beautiful image of Wink Martindale in a checkered suit, asking a contestant a maddeningly easy question. But that night, Rocco woke me up with bad news. He told me he couldn't go through with the appeal. He'd been in the joint so long, he was downright institutionalized. He confessed that he was afraid of freedom. I couldn't understand where he was coming from. I missed my freedom more than anything. I loved my freedom. And here in the hoosegow, they were pretty stingy when it came to any freedom whatsoever.

Then Rocco explained the difference between the outside and the inside to me. On the outside, a man rises to power using his ambition and cunning. On the inside, you make your way up the ropes one way and one way only: by the number of fellows you can rape.

That's why, within the jail, Rocco's name was spoken in hushed tones. He was a raper's raper. He was staying right here in prison, he told me, because inside he had the necessary skills to command respect and prestige, but outside he was a nobody. I was no longer his lawyer, just another prisoner, and if I knew what was good for me I'd better start raping.

Now, I'd never raped anybody before, and in the free world I had worn that fact as a badge of honor, mentioning it proudly and loudly at dinner parties and social events. Folks admired me for it.

"Say what you will about old Norm," my friends would often say, "but he won't rape you!" Every time I heard that, it'd make me feel good inside, like a warm shot of whiskey. But here in the penitentiary, the rules had been turned upside down.

I wanted to fit in, but the problem was that I didn't care much for sex with men. I liked men fine when it came to watching football games with them, and eating Cheetos, and playing videogames, but when it came to having sex with them, I'd just had to grin and bear it.

"You've got it all wrong, Norm," Rocco explained. "Rape has nothing to do with sex. It's all about power, buddy."

I gotta admit, when Rocco first told me that, I thought it was about the damnfoolest thing a man could say. But the more I chewed on it, the more sense it started to make. Rape was all about making the other guy feel small; then I'd look big and strong beside him. I'd done similar things in the free world plenty—spraying a handful of quarters onto a busy thoroughfare and laughing as the homeless bums dodged cars and trucks to earn their supper. I had always felt really big inside when I'd done that. And, apparently, that's what raping a fellow in prison felt like, or so Rocco told me.

So I made up my mind then and there that as soon as the opportunity availed itself I would take ungentlemanly advantage of some hapless prisoner. I got my opportunity while I was working one night in the machine shop and I looked over and there stood Marvin Adelman. Marvin was doing a five-year bid for securities and exchange fraud. He had large black glasses, thinning gray hair, and whiskers that made him look just like a rodent with large black glasses.

I shouted at him loud, so all my fellow inmates could hear. "Hey, Adelman, I'm going to rape you the same way you raped the people who invested all their money in your Ponzi schemes. The only difference is, whereas you raped them in a metaphorical sense, I'm setting out to—" I stopped my speech. Marvin had fled. I had made the biggest mistake of the novice raper: I had made my intentions known.

The whole yard laughed at me as I turned beet red. I took off in an embarrassed rage, determined that I would rape Marvin Adelman before the sun touched the horizon.

It took a while, but I finally located Marvin cowering behind a belt sander. This was a good sign. Whenever a guy is cowering, you know that you have the upper hand. I started chasing him, but he was fast and elusive, like a jackrabbit wearing large black glasses. I'd run at him full speed, thinking I finally had him, but at the last moment he'd duck to his left or his right, and I'd go crashing into a wall. I was dog-tired and gasping heavily when I finally got him cornered, and as I made a final lunge toward him I tripped and hit my head on a belt sander.

I don't know how long I was out, but when I regained consciousness the first thing I heard was the laughter. I looked around and all the prisoners were beside themselves with delight, laughing and poking each other in the sides. The only man who was not laughing was

Rocco. He sat in a chair way in the back, but he was close enough that I could see the disappointment in his eyes. I couldn't make sense of any of it, but then I turned around and saw what had the boys in the black-and-white pajamas convulsing in this mass paroxysm of mirth.

There, behind me, was Marvin Edelman—all hundred thirty pounds of him—and what do you suppose Marvin was doing that was so funny that he had everybody busting a gut? Well, he was raping me, that's what! He was raping the hell out of me. You know, I had never understood the concept of irony before, but I guessed that this was it, all right, and I was not a fan. "Get the hell off me, Adelman, and enough with the raping!" I said.

"Why should I?"

"Yeah, why should he?" the prisoners repeated as one.

I was starting to feel pretty powerless, so I had to think and think fast.

"I'll tell you why," I said. "Because if you don't cut out the raping, and pronto, I'll go to my cell and get my handmade knife and that'll be the end of you." (I made a mental note to fashion myself a handmade knife when I got back to my cell.) "But I'm willing to make a deal with you, Adelman. We are both civilized men. You quit raping me right now and there'll be no hard feelings. And you won't see a reprisal rape outta me either, I promise you that."

Marvin stopped his raping for a minute, and I could see by the look on his face he was turning the offer over in his mind. "I don't know," he said. "I kinda like this feeling of power."

"But rape isn't about power, Marvin. You've got it all wrong. It's about sex, don't you see?"

I could tell this was confusing Marvin, and that gave me just the time I needed. I slammed my elbow into his spectacles.

"I'm blind, I'm blind!" he screamed.

"And you're raped as well!" I said triumphantly, and I began my savage reprisal rape of Marvin Adelman, prisoner 6020311.

"Now who's raping whom?" I asked.

Adelman must have thought this was a rhetorical question, because he just whimpered and cried and my non-rhetorical question hung awkwardly in the air, unanswered, before I proclaimed, "I'm raping you, that's who."

Just then a guard showed up. "You've done your time, Macdonald. You're free to go."

"I am?" I asked. "I thought I was in for forty years."

"Nope, four months."

"Well, I'll be damned."

We all had a good laugh at that one.

I was not always a ghost. As with all ghosts, I was once a living, breathing man. I lived in the city by the bay, and in a coffeehouse I sat at the feet of the masters and listened. There was Neal Cassady and Kerouac too, and Ginsberg, who howled at the moon. They were beautiful and they were my family. Now they are all ghosts, just like me. Only difference is, I'm alive.

They were the young lions of Beat, but their time was growing short when I arrived in the city. They had been replaced by hippies, who wore bright colors and danced and did psychedelic drugs. The year was 1966, and I had decided I would be the beatniks' biographer. I knew them all, I loved them, and I would write a book about these titans and let the world know these men, how they lived like no others, how they shook the literary world to its foundation.

And so I shadowed them everywhere and asked them everything, and their answers were the greatest education a young writer could hope to receive. Burroughs, Kerouac, and Ginsberg were my main subjects.

Julie Grau, a family friend who was working as a reader at Random House and was the first to believe in me, said that I had written a classic work of nonfiction and soon my name would be known throughout the country. Unfortunately, Julie was right on both counts.

I had grown very close to my subjects. Yes, they were geniuses, but to me they were family, and so I decided to name the book My Beautiful Family.

Random House sent the advance copies out to the critics, and every single one heaped lavish praise on me. They heralded me as the next great American voice and called the book a masterpiece. I could not believe it. At twenty years of age, I was sure to become the toast of the literary world. They all agreed with Julie that my name was about to become famous. And they were right as well.

You see, my name was not Terence Keane at the time. But, oh, how I wish that this had been my real name back then. Because when my work hit the bookshelves in late November of 1969, it contained the cursed name I was given at birth, a name unknown when the book was published but widely known only days later. I will never forget the elation I felt when, early on the morning of November 29, I looked through the window of Rizzoli's on 57th Street and saw dozens of copies of my book on prominent display.

There it was.

My Beautiful Family *by Charles Manson.*

20

THE DEVIL, YOU SAY

"So, Norm, how come you were only in prison for four months when you thought you were in for forty years?"

"Well, Adam Eget," I say, "I just didn't hear right. The judge had given me a sentence of four months. But I thought he'd given me forty years, which is longer.

"I'd played it right, though. I'd taken care of Lorne even from jail. He'd visit me every week at Rikers and he'd always leave a few grains heavier."

"But how did the show cover all that time you were gone, Norm?"

"That was just dumb luck. I'd only been on the show a handful of episodes and nobody knew who I was when I was sent away. When I got out I had three shows to go in the first season to prove myself, and I was determined to be a star. I should have been having the time of my life, wearing free-world clothes and enjoying free-world delights."

"You must have been living it up, huh?"

"No, Adam Eget, not one bit. Sarah never left my mind."

"Don't tell me you kept trying to get her."

"Yes, Adam Eget. And it nearly cost me everything." I know this story will be hard to tell, so I measure out a double shot of morphine and press the syrette smoothly under my tongue. And once again the present becomes the past.

I was sitting at the bar, drinking Wild Turkey 101 and talking aloud to myself. "It's not fair. I'd do anything to have Sarah for my very own."

"Anything?" whispered a voice to my right, and I turned and faced the sneering smile and merry, wicked eyes of a stranger sitting next to me.

"Yeah, sure, stranger," I said. "Why, I'd give up anything if only Sarah would love me the way that I love her."

"Perhaps I could be of service," the stranger said, and he threw his head back and roared a loud, mirthless laugh that filled the room.

"Whatcha laughing at, mister?" I said. "I mean, no offense, but I've heard better jokes."

His yellow eyes narrowed and hardened. "Do you not know who I am?" he hissed, and a vague whiff of sulfur touched my nose.

"Well, you're not Bob Hope, I'll tell you that. I mean, that joke fell flat, mister. You were the only one in the whole joint laughing. It was downright embarrassing."

"Silence!" bellowed the stranger, and now the sulfur fully invaded my nostrils and I choked. "I have been called by many names. Perhaps you know me as Lucifer, Mephistopheles, the Prince of Darkness, Beelzebub, Old Scratch, the Lord Host of the Hoary Netherworld, the Beast, the Archfiend, the Father of All Lies, the Great Deceiver, the Fallen Angel. I'm Satan himself."

"Sorry, buddy, never heard of you," I said as I turned back to my half-finished Wild Turkey 101.

"I'm the Devil, you moron," he said.

So that was it. The Devil. It all made sense now. The stench of brimstone, his wolfish yellow eyes and teeth, the red pitchfork leaning against his barstool.

"I can make it so that this Sarah girl will love you with all her heart," said the Unholy One. "Sign this and she is yours."

The Devil produced a parchment, tattered, yellow, and ancient, and placed it before me on the bar. It read: "The one you love will love you forever. In exchange, you agree to give to the Devil your immortal soul. Plus two beers."

I then read the small print. "The beers shall be Pabst Blue Ribbon. If they are out of Pabst Blue Ribbon, as is often the case in this particular establishment, then you shall give the Devil your immortal soul. Plus two of whatever's on draft."

The price seemed a mite steep to me, but then I thought about how I hadn't lived such an upright life and that if I refused the deal but ended up down there anyhow, with the Devil raping me for all of time, I'd feel like a right fool.

"I'll do it," I said.

The Devil scratched my fingertip with his claw, and blood pooled there as I shuddered and signed the hellish contract. I looked up at the Dark One, but just as he had suddenly appeared, so now he had suddenly vanished. Into the men's room.

I settled up with the barkeep: six shots of Wild Turkey 101 that I'd drunk and two Pabst Blue Ribbons for Old Ned.

Two weeks went by and I didn't see Sarah. Normally a fortnight away from my one true love would have me pacing back and forth in my room like those big cats in the small cages over at the Central Park Zoo. But the funny thing is that when you know a girl loves you more than life itself, you can afford to play it cool. Real cool.

When I finally broke and arrived at her threshold, Sarah looked surprised. "I don't know what to say, Norm," she stuttered. But words were needless now. Her eyes spoke to me of yearning, of want, and of need.

I took Sarah into my arms and kissed her deep and then deeper again. But no tongue. This was love, after all. The kiss calmed my doomed soul and I felt like I was floating, calm, and everything was right in the world. Then I heard the hissing.

It was steady, slow, and unrelenting. I recognized the sound immediately, as I had heard it many, many times before. It was the sound of Mace.

My eyes and lungs filled with the stuff as I stumbled, blind and choking. When the sound finally ceased, I fell backward and hit the back of my head on something hard. I couldn't see or talk, but I could hear just fine. And what I heard was the sound of a purse being rummaged through and then the unmistakable sound of another can of Mace being opened. Then the hissing began again and I scrabbled backward into a wall as I tried vainly to endure the spray of fire. By my estimate the first assault had only been about a third of a can. This full can would be much, much worse. Three times as bad, if my calculations were correct. I could only hope that Sarah had escaped.

I lost consciousness somewhere during all of this, but I'm here to tell you that nothing will wake you up faster than being thrown off a second-story balcony. I suppose I was lucky a cement alleyway was there to break my fall but, still, it hurt. It hurt like a bastard. I looked up at the balcony and my beautiful Sarah was there. I was so happy she was okay, and not only was she okay, she was laughing. Well, that got me laughing too, although my laugh came out like a loose rattle and sprayed blood on the cement. That made Sarah laugh even harder.

"Love sure is funny, isn't it, Sarah?" I croaked. "One second you're kissing and being in love and all, and the next second some guy breaks into your apartment and starts Macing you and the fellow you love."

"I don't love you, Norm. I hate your guts."

I looked up at Sarah and instantly understood she was telling the truth. She did hate my guts. But she wasn't to blame. I was sure that

Dave Attell had made his own diabolical deal. My quarrel was now with the Devil himself.

I dragged my broken body to the tavern, ordered a whiskey, and asked the barkeep where I could find the Devil. He looked at me funny.

"He was in here a couple weeks back," I said. "Yellow wolfish eyes, diabolical laugh, carries a trident."

"Oh, you must be talking about Phil Bradshaw," said the barkeep.

"He goes by many a name," I said. "Have you seen him?"

"Bradshaw!" hollered the barkeep. "Man out here looking for you."

I spotted the Fallen One in the corner, playing a game of Ms. Pac-Man and nursing a Pabst Blue Ribbon.

A *Pabst Blue Ribbon*, I thought to myself. *That means some other poor fool lost his soul tonight.*

"Well, well, well!" I shouted angrily. "If it isn't the Devil himself!"

"Where? Where?" the Devil cried, looking first here, then there, searching the room. I saw a look of wild alarm in his lupine eyes.

"Enough of your malarkey, Devil. You reneged on your promise. My true love loves me not. And the way I see it, that means this contract is null and void." I pulled out the ancient parchment with my bloody signature.

The Devil regained his calm and looked up at me from his chair. He took the document and pulled out some reading glasses. "So she doesn't love you back, huh?"

"No, Sarah Silverman has nothing but ice in her heart for me."

"Sarah Silverman?" asked the Devil. "That's the girl who doesn't love you back?"

"Yeah."

"Well, you never told me it was Sarah Silverman. What are you, nuts? She's way outta your league, pal. Listen, I'll tell you what I'll do. There's a girl who starts work here in about an hour. Sure, she's a little hefty and her face isn't much to look at, but she's got real nice long hair. Now, if you were to sign another contract, she will be yours forever." And then he began his demoniacal laugh but quickly thought better of it and pretended he was coughing.

"You failed in your task, Evil One, and so you must destroy this infernal contract and return to me my immortal soul," I insisted.

"Trouble over there, Bradshaw?" I heard the barkeep yell across the room.

"No, no. Everything's just fine, Mr. Billingsly. No trouble at all."

"Make sure you keep it that way."

"Yes, Mr. Billingsly. You bet. You won't hear a peep out of me."

The Devil turned to me, and I saw he was suppressing his otherworldly rage. "Now, look, if Sarah Silverman doesn't love you, then it is true, I am technically in breach of this contract, but, you see, there's a problem."

I gulped with fear. "What's the problem?"

"The two beers. I can't swing it today. Best I can do is give you this one, but it's half empty. Otherwise it might take me five, six days to get my hands on two beers. I haven't been making many deals lately. People are less and less ambitious. They're willing to settle, I guess. At least in this neighborhood."

I looked in his evil eyes with dread. "So my soul is yours?" I wept.

"Your soul? Oh, right, your soul. Well, I'll tell you what. How about I give you back your immortal soul, we forget all about the two beers, and I'll burn that contract right now." He grabbed the parchment, borrowed a lighter from a nearby patron, and set it ablaze.

My heart was filled with joy. True, I didn't win the love of Sarah Silverman—although I continued to try each day via unanswered phone calls, unanswered emails, unanswered yelling at her apartment door—but not everyone can say they beat the Devil.

21

THE LOST DAYS

I awaken from my blackout without hangover. As always, I feel fresh as a newborn. Of course, I have no memory, only the knowledge that I was happy where I was and now am sad that I am back, in the way that a man, upon awakening, will feel nostalgia for his wonderful dream, even though it is forgotten before his feet hit the hard floor of his hard house. I know time has passed and I know that I am lying fully clothed in a bathtub. I am cold and it is hard to get up and stand. When I finally manage it, I look in the full-length mirror and am shocked. My face has some scabs, the small kind you get from falling on pavement, and I am bruised about the jaw and cheekbones. But I have come out of blackouts worse than that. What alarms me is that I am now a big fat guy. I have to have gained seventy-five pounds.

"Adam Eget!" I scream, and he comes in from the other room. I ask him the date and he tells me.

"That's over a month. Over a month I've been blacked out?" A month is a long time, and it feels even longer in Las Vegas, where a lot can change in very little time. "Tell me what happened, Adam Eget. How bad was it?"

Adam Eget yawns. "Are you kidding? You couldn't lose. You don't remember it at all?"

"No, none of it," I laugh. "But from the look of my round belly and my extra chin, I'm a prosperous man!" I laugh some more and dance around the room. "I'm gonna hit the tables. Where the hell's my money?"

"I'm sorry, Norm, but Gabe insisted all the money be kept in the safe."

"Haha, well, don't worry about it, friend. Gabe is a smart man," I say. "Come and sit, now, Adam Eget, and tell me exactly what I have been up to this past month."

I sit on the edge of a chair and listen to my forgotten adventure. And what a picture Adam Eget paints. I had visited every casino on the strip with my two pals in tow. I had taken up with a beautiful Cree girl that I was set to marry, but then I got cold feet and may have lost the love of my life. I had outdrunk a local pimp, who then went after me with a knife and almost killed me, but Gabe had used martial arts on this gentleman of leisure and for that I owed him my life. I finally ended up here at Harrah's, where I'd been the talk of the floor, a man blind drunk who couldn't lose, who would hit 19 and find a 2. It all sounds wonderful, but part of me is sad. Sad that it is another splinter of my life that has happened and I will never re-member it. Another splinter that I have to take another person's word for.

"I'm gonna quit drinking and be just like you, Adam Eget." We both laugh hard at that one.

As we dance and laugh, Gabe walks in and he is carrying two bags from 7-Eleven. He empties them into the middle of the room. Food spills everywhere. There are Twizzlers and Butterfingers and Rolos and Creamsicles and PayDays and more and more and more.

"There you go, Fatso. That oughta hold you for a while."

"He's back, Gabe. He's back."

"Yeah, I'm back," I say. "I'm sorry I missed out on all the fun. Adam Eget says we've been to every casino in town."

"Yep," says Gabe.

"Listen, Gabe, I really want to thank you for taking care of that knife-wielding pimp I outdrank."

"Don't mention it. I've never liked pimps," says Gabe. "Love should never be for sale." Gabe is always saying wise words like these, words that you'd expect to see on a T-shirt or a coffee mug.

I want to know if I'd made the million yet and, if not, how close I am. "How much did I win, Gabe, how much did I win?"

Gabe just looks at me. "How much did you win? You black out on whiskey and expect to wake up in a bed of cash? No. You wake up in a cold, hard bathtub, which is what you did."

"But Adam Eget told me I couldn't lose."

Adam Eget has two Entenmann's donuts in his mouth. "Oh, I was just talking about last night, Norm. You couldn't lose last night. Sorry for the misunderstanding."

"SORRY FOR THE MISUNDERSTANDING?" I leap across the room and am on Adam Eget and choking him, but his ubiquitous sweat protects him. It is like trying to keep hold of a greased pig. But I stay on top of him and finally have him pinned to the floor. I'm throwing punches and Adam Eget is whimpering and crying and I keep screaming, "SORRY FOR THE MISUNDERSTANDING?" I feel Gabe on my back, trying to pry me loose, but my enormous girth prevents anything of the sort. It seems like Adam Eget is certain to die by my hand, but Gabe finally hits me across the back with a chair. The chair does not smash to pieces like in the movies, so he just keeps hitting me with it until finally I roll over, finished. Gabe places the chair back where he found it. The chair looks fine; it hasn't lost a single splinter. I can barely breathe.

"Where do I stand, Gabe?"

"You've worn out your credit at every casino. You owe a million and you have roughly seventy thousand from your hot streak last night."

I try to get up, but I'm not used to all the extra weight and my knees buckle. I crawl to the candy and empty a pack of Junior Mints in my mouth, then begin to unwrap a Butterfinger. "Why am I eating like this, Gabe? What's going on?"

"I've been thinking on that," says Gabe. "Did you ever see the movie *Milk*?"

"I love milk," says Adam Eget.

"Right," Gabe says, "but, you mean you love to drink it out of a glass or maybe put it on your cereal."

"Oh, yes," says Adam Eget.

"Well, this movie, *Milk*, it has nothing to do with that. It's about a politician in San Francisco who is killed by this crazy guy. And it was a true story. So when this guy goes on trial, the media dubs it 'the Twinkie defense' 'cause this crazy guy ate a lot of Twinkies. But the media had it all wrong. They said the defense was claiming eating Twinkies made their client crazy. What the defense was really saying was that eating a lot of junk food was a symptom of mental illness. That when you're going crazy, your brain craves sugar."

"Gabe, you trying to tell me I went crazy?"

"You went crazy and you went fat."

"I can still win, Gabe."

Gabe puts his mouth close to my ear. "It may be time to begin readying yourself for Plan B."

Adam Eget and I take the last seventy thousand over to the craps table. I bet five thousand on every number, so I have thirty thousand dollars on the table. I know as I do it I am out of control, but I cannot stop. Gabe was right. I'm still on tilt. My only hope now is to hit a run of good luck. Hitting a run of good luck at the exact time you are on tilt can make you a fortune fast. But instead I watch as my bankroll goes up, then down, then up again, and I think how this will likely be the last time I place money on a game of chance.

I remember a psychiatrist once telling me that I gamble in order to escape the reality of life, and I told him that's why everyone does everything. But I've had plenty of wasted nights, after losses and bigger losses, to consider the question more seriously. So why the attraction? Most people would think it's the wins that keep the gambler going, but any gambler knows this is not true. As you place your chips on the craps table, you feel anxiety and impatience. When the red dice hit the green felt with a thunk and you're declared the winner and the chips are pushed toward you, you feel relief. Relief is all. And relief is fine, but hardly what a man would give the whole rest of his life to gain. It has to be something else, and the best I've come up with is this: It is a particular moment. A magic moment that occurs after the placing of a bet and before the result of that bet. It is after the red dice are thrown but before they lie still on the green felt where they fall. It is when the dice are in the air, and as long as they are there, time stops. As long as the red dice are in the air, the gambler has hope. And hope is a wonderful thing to be addicted to.

"Better luck next time, sir."

In a casino, these are the words that tell you that you are broke. "Better luck next time, sir." I stumble over to a chair by the slots. I light a cigarette and take a deep drag. When the casino takes all I have, I usually feel lost and don't know what to do. But this time is different. I know exactly what to do. I have Plan B.

I find Adam Eget by the video keno machine and take the news that he is up a dollar and eighty-five cents in stride. "Adam Eget, listen to me. Go now and find the man you think is a lady and stay with her somewhere downtown. Somewhere you will be noticed. Start a fight in public. Make yourself seen. Tomorrow evening, return here and find me in my bed."

"Gotcha, boss." And Adam Eget turns on his heel to leave.

"Whoa, whoa, whoa, whoa. That's it? That's all you have to say?"

"Yeah, I mean, I'm gonna see you tomorrow night."

"You never really understood Plan B, did you, Adam Eget?"

"Not really."

And so I have to explain the plan again to Adam Eget, and when he finally understands it, he begins to weep like a woman and asks me to promise that I will do no harm to myself.

"I will not promise that, Adam Eget. It goes against everything Plan B stands for. But remember this: When you come back tomorrow, it will not be me you find in the hotel room bed"—and then I have him touch the flesh of my arm and the bones underneath—"but only these clothes I wear."

Adam Eget goes off into the night and I go to my room.

I sit on the edge of my bed and open the drawer. I take out the 600 milligrams of Dilaudid, the fresh syrette, and the Gideon's Bible. I read a few of my favorite Scripture passages as I prepare the syrettes. And then I inject myself with the lethal dose of Dilaudid. I fall to my knees and rest my elbows on the bed. I pray forgiveness for what I am doing. And then I feel joy and peace fill my soul as my consciousness quietly drifts away.

And then . . . I don't die.

22

MEETING GOD

I find my way through the casino and in a moment I am on the Strip. There is a dry chill that begins to freeze my naked face, and the buildings of iron and glass feel as immortal as the ancient streets they sit upon. I look above and the sun shining amid the blue sky and white, white clouds casts a pall of futility over the man-made monuments and their sickly neon light.

And I stand by the Pyramid of Luxor and gaze upon the firmament above, and in a sudden the sky becomes a face and I look away in fear and shame.

It is the face of God and He speaks, and His voice is both yours and mine at once, and He speaks unto me.

"WHY DO YOU NOT LOOK AT ME, NEITHER YESTER-DAY NOR TODAY?" And so I remove my *Dirty Work* hat and look upon Him and study His countenance.

Now, people always wonder if God is a man or a woman or black or white or yellow, but I'm here to tell you that none of this silly stuff matters. (He's a white guy, by the way.) What matters is how truly big He is. He is bigger than the cities, than the world, than the sun. He is bigger than your hopes, your imaginings, your dreams, and even your ambitions. Plus He has a mustache.

And when I lock eyes with this supernatural giant, I feel the emptiness that I have always carried deep in my gut vanish, and a sudden quiet peace replaces it.

"WAIT A MINUTE—YOUR EYES ARE WEIRD; THE PUPILS ARE ALL DILATED. YOU AREN'T STONED, ARE YOU?" God looks concerned, and He moves His face close to inspect me.

"No."

"ARE YOU SURE? 'CAUSE YOU LOOK REALLY STONED."

"No. I mean . . . Oh, yeah, kinda."

God throws up His hands and shakes His head in exasperation. "WELL, THAT'S JUST GREAT. BECAUSE I HAVE COME TO YOU WITH A MESSAGE FOR THE PEOPLE OF EARTH, AND WHO BETTER TO DELIVER MY MESSAGE TO THE PEOPLE OF EARTH THAN A STONED GUY. DOESN'T GET ANY MORE CONVINCING THAN THAT."

"Look, Lord, there's no need for sarcasm. Listen, maybe you should find someone else. I'm just a nightclub comic who travels across the country and gives people the gift of happiness with jokes about answering machines. I'm sure I'll go to heaven, right?"

"FINE, I'LL FIND ANOTHER. AS FAR AS GOING TO HEAVEN, I CAN'T SAY."

Well, that really scares me, so I think fast. "Hold on, hold on. It was only a joke! Of course I'm your guy. I'm your guy. I was kidding earlier when I said you should find someone else. It's so funny that you thought I was being serious, because I was totally kidding."

And the Lord begins to speak His message, but just as He begins, a second wave of the drug hits me, much harder, and the sidewalk becomes quicksand beneath my feet and I sink into it, fast. I clutch at a lamppost and hold on hard so that the sidewalk does not swallow me and fill my lungs with sand. Around me I see, in a circle that grows ever smaller, a pack of wildcats sauntering nearer and nearer, and their green eyes shine and their white teeth are slick with saliva and their breath can be seen in the cold, cold air. Time that is beyond all human calculation passes, and a crash of thunder makes the mountain cats race up to the top of the Luxor hotel, where they fasten themselves like gargoyles to the top of the pyramid. I am alone now but for Him. I look up and He is making pronouncements, and He looks mighty and self-satisfied too.

"... AND IT HAS TO BE IN THOSE EXACT WORDS. NOW REPEAT THEM BACK TO ME."

And I say, "I'm sorry, man, some weird shit was going down. I wasn't listening."

"OH, WELL, THAT'S COOL, DON'T WORRY ABOUT IT." But I can see that He is sulking.

"Hold on, I'll get a pencil!" I race to the Luxor's gift shop to buy a pencil and a notebook from a half-man half-alligator, and I am now ready to write down all His words, the better to convey them to the people of earth.

"SAY UNTO THEM, REDEMPTION IS NEAR!"

"Got it. Redaction is near."

"REDEMPTION!!"

"Revenging."

"REDEMPTION!!!"

"Got it," I say again. "Got it." I look down and the pencil is the finger of a dead woman and it is blue-black.

"AND THE PERFIDY OF MAN . . ."

"And the ferfectly on man."

"NO! NO! THAT'S NOT EVEN A WORD. JUST FOCUS." I can tell that God is getting very frustrated, but it isn't my fault. God knows way more words than I do.

And on it goes, with Him making pronouncements and using very difficult words, and then me getting something wrong, and Him getting all disappointed in me, until finally it ends.

"AND SUCH IS THE WAY TO ETERNAL BLISS."

"Got it, Chief!" I say, and place my notebook and the dead woman's finger in my pocket.

"WELL?"

"Well what?" I say.

"WELL, WHAT DO YOU THINK OF MY SPEECH TO THE PEOPLE OF EARTH?"

"I'm sorry, but I was transcribing it, so I wasn't really listening. I can't do both."

He is about to begin sulking again, so I quickly say, "But you know what? I'm sure it's just great."

"YEAH, RIGHT." There's that sarcasm, but I can tell I've hurt His feelings as well. I guess everyone wants to be heard, even if it's your own Creator. And His face is gone, and where it had been lies the sky and on the sky lie the clouds and the moon and the stars.

I look down at my scribbling and can't make out a word of it, due to my awful handwriting. It's too bad, but I can't do anything about it now, so I crumple up the paper and throw it on the sidewalk and it bursts into a jagged flame and thunder crashes in my ear. I know that He is not at all cool with my crumpling of His message, and I am afraid. That piece of paper had words upon it that would save the souls of all men, and I could have been the one to deliver them to the world. I could have spoken to all of mankind, and my name would have been one with Abraham, and Moses, and David.

It's depressing, but that is not to be. And so I wander back to my hotel room and watch *Tank Girl* four times back-to-back.

On November 30, 1969, Charles Day reviewed my book in The New York Times Book Review.

"I have just heard the freshest voice in the last fifty years. It belongs to a young man named Charles Manson, and in his debut work he examines the life and work of this generation's most talented and influential writers. With his dizzying style and 'you didn't have to be there' storytelling perfection, Charles Manson draws a perfectly observed portrait of the scene that produced the most famous Beat artists. Charles Manson has a reckless style, cutting and dangerous, and he is happily willing to break every convention our literary society holds sacred. Yes, Charles Manson is dangerous, no question, but he also has a charisma that makes one forgive his savage style. I can assert without hesitation that My Beautiful Family *is the best work, fiction or nonfiction, to be written in the last decade. It is a masterpiece that will live forever, and its author will be worshipped. The name Charles Manson may not be well known now, but, trust me, it soon will be."*

And it soon was. Two days after the review, the LAPD alleged that a small, clownish, deranged man had overseen an orgy of murder that had kept the nation in terror during the summer of hate in 1969. His name was Charles Manson, and he was charged with the murder of seven people. But there was an eighth victim, and his name was Charles Manson. Not the Charles Manson who had overseen an orgy of murder that kept the nation in terror during the summer of hate in 1969—the other Charles Manson. Me.

The next day, My Beautiful Family *by Charles Manson was removed from every bookstore in the country. I stood with Julie Grau in Columbus Circle and watched as copy after copy of my book was thrown into a large bonfire.*

23

MAKE A WISH

dam Eget walks in, sees me watching *Tank Girl,* and faints. I revive him and he begins jumping up and down and shouting, "You're alive! You're alive!" He tries to hug me but can't get his arms all the way around due to my girth, so it is only half a hug.

I laugh. "Yes, Adam Eget, I am alive. I felt this life had nothing left to offer but I was wrong. Life offers the squeals of delight as you pass a park filled with children. Life offers breakfast with a friend, drinking coffee and laughing at past mistakes. Life offers the kiss of a stranger, unexpected and thrilling. Life offers Dilaudid. What a wonderful life I almost tossed away."

Adam Eget suddenly becomes serious. "Norm, when I thought that you had died, I wondered if you were in heaven or the other place. What do you think, Norm, will we go to heaven? Are we good men?" The question stops me cold. I know we are not truly good men, but I cannot tell Adam Eget that.

"Sure, we are good. We saved a young boy, didn't we? We saved a young boy who the doctors said was beyond saving."

I can see Adam Eget is smiling now, and I will need to keep his spirits up. So I remind him of the time we made a young boy's wish come true.

It was the end of my first year on *SNL,* and even if I was never really on the show, just the fact that I was brushing up against it was making me a celebrity. And when you are a celebrity, everyone is always bugging you to do things. Good things.

The boy had been alive nine years, which made him young, but he would only be alive for one more year, which made him old. He was in a sad situation and he had a wish that he needed my help to realize. It was a simple wish: to meet me and follow me around for a day at the *Saturday Night Live* TV show. As final wishes go, it seemed like a damned poor one.

So that's why I was walking down a dim green hospital corridor that fine cold New York afternoon instead of being where I should have—pitching my hysterical sketch about answering machines to Lorne Michaels for the following Saturday. But there are some things more important than television programs.

I knew that dragging a terminally ill child around the studio for a whole day was sure to make me the laughingstock of my co-workers and could potentially get me fired, but sometimes you have to look at the big picture. The truth was, I had not lived an upright life, what with the shoplifting, the adultery, the taking of the Lord's name in vain, the coveting of my neighbor's ox (Goddammit, I loved that ox), and the worshipping of that golden calf every time God didn't answer one of my countless prayers. I needed to do something exceptionally selfless to even up the books come Judgment Day and keep me from the Devil's grasp for all of eternity. Making this boy's wish come true seemed like it just might do the trick.

I don't much like hospitals, and I said as much when I met the boy's physician. "You may as well know, Doc, I'm no fan of diseases, and I'll never understand filling a whole building with them."

"What are you, an idiot?" said the doctor.

"Yeah, I'm an idiot, all right. An idiot just like Alfred Einstein. I'll have you know that I'm Norm Macdonald and I work on the *Saturday Night Live* TV show, and I am a bigshot."

"*Saturday Night Live*? That show hasn't been funny since Bill Murray left."

A crowd was beginning to form, which was perfect for me since I was a stand-up comedian. I decided I would put this doctor in his place.

"If you think it's so easy being funny, Doc, then why don't you tell us all a joke?"

So he did.

And it was one of the funniest jokes I'd ever heard. I'll never forget it. His timing was flawless.

A moth goes into a podiatrist's office. The podiatrist says, "What's the problem?"

The moth says, "Where do I begin with my problems? Every day I go to work for Gregory Vassilievich, and all day long I toil. But what is my work? I am a bureaucrat, and so every day I joylessly move papers from one place to another and then back again. I no longer know what it is that I actually do, and I don't even know if Gregory Vassilievich knows. He only knows that he has power over me, and this seems to bring him much happiness. And where is my happiness? It is when I awake in the morning and I do not know who I am. In that single moment I am happy. In that single moment, before the memory of who I am strikes me like a cane. And I take to the streets and walk, in a malaise, here and then there and then here again. And then it is time for work. Others stopped asking me what I do for a living long ago, for they know I will have no answer and will fix my empty eyes upon them, and they fear my melancholia might prove so deep as to be contagious. Sometimes, Doc, in the deep-est dark of night, I awake in my bed and I turn to my right, and with horror I see some old lady lying on my arm. An old lady that I once loved, Doc, in whose flesh I once found splendor and now see only decay, an old lady who insults me by her very existence.

"Once, Doc, when I was young, I flew into a spiderweb and was trapped. In my panic, I smashed my wings till the dust flew from them, but it did not free me and only alerted the spider. The spider moved toward me and I became still, and the spider stopped. I had heard many stories from my elders about spiders, about how they would sink their fangs into your cephalotho-rax and you would be paralyzed but aware as the spider slowly devoured you. So I remained as still as possible, but when the spider again began moving toward me, I smashed my wing again into my cage of silk, and this time it worked. I cut into the web and freed myself and flew skyward. I was free and filled with joy, but this joy soon turned to horror: I looked down and saw that in my escape I had taken with me a single strand of silk, and at the end of the strand was the spider, who was scrambling upward toward me. Was I to die high in the sky, where no spider should be? I flew this way, then that, and finally I freed myself from the strand and watched as it floated earthward with the spider. But days later a strange feeling descended upon my soul, Doc. I began to feel that my life was that single strand of silk, with a deadly spider racing up it and toward me. And I felt that I had already been bitten by his venomous fangs and that I was living in a state of paralysis, as life devoured me whole.

"My daughter, Alexandria, fell to the cold of last winter. The cold took her, as it did many of us. And so my family mourned. And I placed on my countenance the look of grief, Doc, but it was a masquerade. I felt no grief for my dead daughter but only envy. And so I have one child now, a boy, whose name is Stephan Mikhailovitch Smokovnikov, and I tell you now, Doc, with great and deep shame, the terrible truth. I no longer love him. When I look into his eyes, all I see is the same cowardice that I see when I catch a glimpse of my own eyes in a mirror. It is this cowardice that keeps me living, Doc, that keeps me moving from place to place, saying hello and goodbye, eating though hunger has long left me, walking without destination, and, at night, lying beside the strange old lady in this burlesque of a life I endure. If only the cowardice would abate for the time needed to reach over and pick up the cocked and loaded pistol that lies on my bedside table, then I might finally end this façade once and for all. But, alas, the cowardice takes no breaks; it is what defines me, it is what frames my life, it is what I am. And yet I cannot resign myself to my own life. Instead, despair is my constant companion as I walk here and then there, without dreams, without hope, and without love."

"Moth," says the podiatrist, "your tale has moved me and it is clear you need help, but it is help I cannot provide. You must see a psychiatrist and tell him of your troubles. Why on earth did you come to my office?"

The moth says, "Because the light was on."

By the end of the joke, everyone around was laughing hard, and I started to laugh too in spite of myself. But then I got angry because I realized that he was making me look small. So I took a swing at him, but I missed by a good foot or so and ended up knocking over an old man who was pushing some futuristic contraption that rolled on wheels and was attached to his right arm by a thin tube. I bent down to apologize, because I felt that the accident was partially my fault, and that's when the doctor kicked me heavy in the ribs.

"I can mend them, but I can bust them up too," he said, and that got another big laugh. Everybody thinks they're a comedian. Especially in my line of work.

I lay there gasping as the doctor recounted a few hilarious anecdotes, and once the laughing crowd dispersed, he started telling me about the boy I was visiting and his illness. He used a lot of big words; he was still clearly determined to make me look small, so I interrupted him. "Okay, okay, I get the idea, Doc. You went to school. I only got one question for you. This thing he's got, is it contagious?"

"No, it's not contagious," he said softly. He looked me in the eye and shook his head at me, all sad and weary. "He's just a poor brave child who hasn't got much time." I noticed a tear as it made its way down his cheek. He wasn't such a tough guy anymore or so funny either. That's what separates professional funnymen like me from bums like that doctor.

I crashed into the boy's room with a big smile on my face. Around his bed, nurses and orderlies and a couple of doctors gathered, and they all held clipboards and looked solemn. Death is a funny thing. Not funny haha, like a Woody Allen movie, but funny strange, like a Woody Allen marriage. When it's unexpected, death comes fast like a ravenous wolf and tears open your throat with a merciful fury. But when it's expected, it comes slow and patient like a snake, and the doctor tells you how far away it is and when, exactly, it will be at your door. And when it will be at the foot of your bed. And when it will be on your flesh. It's all right there on their clipboards.

The room was filled with all kinds of whirring and beeping and dinging. "Would somebody turn that doggone noise down?!" I shouted. Of course, I knew that those noises were coming from machines they were using to keep the boy alive, but I also knew I had to make a big entrance, and I didn't want to disappoint. Only the boy laughed, which was fine with me, because he was the most important one there. Besides me.

I told everybody to scram so I could have a word with the boy alone.

"How you feeling, son?"

"How do you think I'm feeling, Einstein?"

I was genuinely touched that the boy knew I was considered a genius at *Saturday Night Live*. He had clearly done his research. But his comment also reminded me I had to get back to Rockefeller Center and convince Lorne to put my Answering Machine sketch on the air that week. "Well, see you later, kid. Just wanted to let you know I'm happy to make your wish come true before you ... before you ... before you ..."

"Do you swear to God you'll make my wish come true, Norm?"

"Oh, I don't think that would be such a good idea."

"Look at me, Norm."

I couldn't help but comply, and as I looked at the boy a curious tenderness overtook me. "I swear to God."

"Good," the boy said, "because I have a very different wish."

"Please don't tell me I have to take you to the show for *two* days."

"I don't want to go to the show at all. It hasn't been funny since Bill Murray left."

"Well, why did you choose me, then?"

"Because you are a Canadian citizen."

I was confused. "Son, I do not understand. What's your wish and what does anything have to do with me being Canadian?"

The boy looked at me directly and I could see the tears fill his eyes. He spoke softly, his voice quavering and unsteady. "I want to kill a baby seal."

24

HEADING NORTH

"This sketch is gonna be big, Lorne, real big. Comedy is about what people relate to, and everybody has an answering machine. My God, did you even read it?"

"Yes, I read it, Norm, but it's hardly a sketch. First of all, the host is barely in it. Sandler and Farley have no lines at all. As far as I can tell, it's just you talking about how you don't answer your phone anymore and how, later, you tell the person who phoned that you never got the message and that they must have left it on someone else's answering machine. Then Sandler and Farley laugh for an uncomfortably long time."

"Right, they laugh for a long time because what I'm saying is really funny."

"Well, wouldn't it be a better idea to let the audience decide whether it's really funny?"

"With all due respect, Lorne, I think that would be the worst thing we could possibly do. Believe me, I've been down that road before."

"The answer is no, Norm."

"Look, there's only a couple of shows left in the season, and if I don't get a sketch on air, I'm worried for my job."

"Well, you should be," said Lorne.

And then it hit me. He'd found out. Lorne Michaels was well connected in this town, and someone must have tipped him off.

"So I'm being punished for making some kid's final wish come true, is that it? Listen, Lorne, it wasn't my idea. It was some lady who phoned me. I'll phone her back right now and tell her it's not a good week because of the Answering Machine sketch."

Lorne's eyes turned misty, like a woman's sometimes do. "No, no, no, Norm. I think you should fulfill this boy's wish, and, don't worry, I'll make sure we get your sketch on air. But it needs a massive rewrite. Work on it with Fred Wolf." Lorne smiled at me and shook my hand. "I'm proud of you, Norm. You're doing a fine thing," and, with that, his eyes turned misty again. He was an odd duck, Lorne Michaels, no doubt about it.

I put Adam Eget on a plane to Gander, Newfoundland, while I hunkered down with Fred Wolf to work on the Answering Machine sketch. Fred was a writer of the highest order whom I had known for years from our stand-up days. I loved Fred's outright disdain for certain hosts. Many times *SNL* would have a very handsome dramatic actor on as a host. An actor who was convinced he was funny. Women are attracted to funny men, it is often said. This is not true. It only appears this way because women laugh at everything a very handsome man says. So this gives the very handsome men the idea that they are funny. This phenomenon made Fred angry and he refused to refer to the handsome hosts by name; instead, he would call them "Face." "Hey, Norm," he'd say, and point to his script. "You think Face will be able to handle this line?" That would always make me bust a gut. Face. Perfect.

Fred was a pro and very patient, and he convinced me that we should have a phone and an answering machine on the set to add verisimilitude to the sketch. We almost got to blows over that point, because I was afraid the devices would draw focus away from me and the jokes I'd been perfecting for years. I'd done the bit onstage over five thousand times, to mixed results, without ever using a phone or an answering-machine prop. But Fred and I finally reached a compromise. The phone and answering machine would appear in the sketch and, in return, we wouldn't come to blows. We both knew Fred Wolf could beat the living bejeezus out of me.

Cheryl the receptionist stuck her head in the office door. "Phone call from your *assistant*, Adam Eget."

"Say, Cheryl, how come when you say the word 'assistant' you use a tone to make it sound as if Adam Eget is not my assistant at all but something different, something unseemly? Why is it when you say the word you make air quotes with your fingers?" I asked.

"Well, I mean, he is your *assistant,* isn't he? I mean, his job is to *assist* you, so that would make him your *assistant,* wouldn't it?"

"No, Cheryl. Adam Eget is not my *assistant* at all. He's my assistant. He assists me all the time. He's never once *assisted* me. You can ask Fred."

"I thought he was your *assistant* too, Norm. I think everyone does."

"Fred, are you telling me that everybody thinks Adam Eget, my assistant, is actually my *assistant* and that he doesn't assist me at all? That what he really does is *assist* me?"

"Yes."

"He's on line one, Norm." And, with that, Cheryl left.

"Adam Eget here, Norm. I found a guy. We can be in and out of here in three days. If it all works out, we'll have you back Saturday afternoon, just in time for dress rehearsal."

"On my way," I said, and hung up.

25

A WISH FULFILLED

As per our plan, the boy informed his parents, who then informed me, that the boy had decided he might like to spend the entire week at *SNL* so he could see how a sketch goes from an idea on paper all the way to a sketch on live television. *Yeah, me and him both.* I agreed, and two hours later we were both on a prop plane to Gander, Newfoundland.

Edward McClintock was a cod fisherman from up Labrador way. Edward's father and his father's father and his father's father's father had all been sealers. Edward was not a sealer, but he killed seals. "The seal and I make our living the same way. Cod. One seal can eat three to four hundred North Atlantic cod a day. And those are cod I can't catch. Do you follow?"

"Yes, sir," I said. "They sound like gluttonous beasts, these seals. I mean, I like a nice piece of cod as much as the next guy, but three to four hundred? Well, that's just eating to eat."

"Speaking of gluttonous beasts, son, your friend has been eating me out of house and home. And he can't hold his drink. I have no use for a man who can't hold his drink," and he motioned toward Adam Eget, who was inert under a quilt beside the fireplace.

He handed me his bottle of Iceberg rum, and I took a swig of it and felt nice and warm inside. "He can be trusted, sir," I said. "He always does what he's told."

"Fair enough. We'll sit right here and we'll drink till dawn while I tell you what we have to do to kill a seal. Then, in the morning, we'll make our way to the floes. But, honestly, I think it's a mistake. I can see that boy and he looks frail. This is going to be a rugged sojourn, and the boy is pale and his eyes are dim."

"The boy is in perfect health!" I said.

And so, as Adam Eget and the boy slept and dreamt, Edward McClintock and I talked into the night, as men will do, and we were warmed by the fireplace and the Iceberg rum.

Finally, dawn came and the boy woke up. He was ghastly pale and Edward McClintock remarked upon it, but when the boy spoke, his enthusiasm for what lay ahead made him appear to be of sound body. He wanted to hear all about the coming adventure, and Edward McClintock said he would tell us soon but didn't want to repeat anything. Then he got up from his chair, walked to the fireplace, and with his heavy boot he kicked Adam Eget awake.

We sat around the kitchen table as Edward McClintock poured us coffee and warned us about the North Atlantic Ocean. "I first traveled this strip of sea as a child, on a dare, in a small rodney made for jigging squid, and by luck I survived. But in my youthful pride I took my survival as a sign of Providence, and instead of kneeling in thanks, I stood tall in vainglory. Well, since then this sea has battered me and froze me. I've lost four toes and a finger and I've been swept under a dozen times. The North Atlantic Ocean, She don't care about you and me and whether we live or die. You remember that, boys, and show Her the respect She's earned."

"Are you going to make those flapjacks today, Eddie?" Adam Eget asked.

"What?" Edward McClintock snapped.

"Those flapjacks sure are good, Eddie. I could eat those forever."

I saw fire in Edward McClintock's cobalt-blue eyes, and I was afraid for Adam Eget, but Edward held himself still until the fire went out. "Yes," he said, "we'll breakfast big this morning; for the next three days we'll be living on herring and rum."

We ate a great large meal, and I felt fat and fine. Then Edward McClintock took us to the boat and we were off to make a young boy's final wish come true. As I looked at the boy, I noticed he was already shivering under his hides, and Edward McClintock had warned us that it would only get colder. I was scared. If the boy didn't live, it was going to look bad for me. Real bad.

Six hours in, the boy developed a fever. Edward McClintock was very concerned and thought we should turn back. But the boy insisted he would be fine.

"Yes, he'll be fine," I said, and gave him his pills. There were so many pills. I let him wash them down with the Iceberg rum.

As we waited to spot a seal, I played a game with the boy. We would look up at the white clouds above and find figures in them. "That one looks like a bird," I said.

"Yeah, it does, and look at that one. It looks like a man rubbing his nose," he returned.

"I don't see it."

"You see the bottom of it. That's the man's chin and then his mouth is wide open." And then I saw it. And we played this game for two days, and we saw alligators and pickles and trees and every sort of thing, all of them white and still and living in the cold and limitless sky.

In the middle of the second day we heard the cries of seals. The boy jumped up, then coughed an awful rattle of a cough and fell back down. We were all pretty well frozen, and I looked over at Adam Eget, whose tears had become ice halfway down his cheeks.

Edward McClintock pulled the boat up and threw out a rope and then took a hammer and smashed a spike into the three-foot-thick ice and anchored us to the berg. The ice had snow on top, so it wasn't slippery, and up ahead we could see men and hear their gunshots. "Damn punks from St. John's with their pistols. That's not how you kill a seal." He took a rucksack from the boat and pulled out a crude ancient weapon. It had a wooden handle and a curved blade at one end. It looked like a cross between a scythe and a bayonet. "This is a hakapik, son. The baby harp, she has a skull as thin as a shadow, and it takes just one blow to fell her. But your strike must find the forehead. Then her eyes will open and be glassy. When you touch the eyes, if they don't move, the beast is dead. Do you follow?"

"Yes, sir," the boy said, and smiled broadly, but then he coughed that awful, empty cough.

We had about one hundred yards between the seal and us, but they were some of the longest yards I've ever traversed. I had to carry the boy toward the seal. There was a wind and it howled like a hammer and I could no longer hear the whimpers of Adam Eget, who slipped and fell every few feet. I hadn't walked for the last two days, and my legs weren't working properly. It was as if I had to learn it new, like a foal, and on snow and ice. I knew I couldn't fall, for the sake of the boy, so I walked slow, stopped to put the boy down and rest every few minutes, and then I began walking again.

We'd only walked about fifty yards when a great weariness settled on me and I didn't think I could go farther. Suddenly all I wanted to do was sleep. But Edward McClintock had warned me that the cold will trick a man and that sleep that sweetly beckons is not really sleep at all but the deeper thing. So I forced my eyes wide and looked ahead, where I saw Edward McClintock, about thirty yards beyond us, standing still as a rabbit. He turned and fastened his malamute eyes on me, and his voice was clock-steady as the frozen words came from his cracked lips: "Baby harp."

Knowing the creature was only some fifty yards from where I

stood gave me the strength to continue. I put the boy down gently, like a kitten, and Edward McClintock handed him the hakapik.

"Are you sure you can swing it, son, or should I help?" he asked, but the boy was already on his way and soon he was standing above the baby seal. We watched, the three of us, while the boy mustered all his strength to swing the hakapik high in the air, then downward and fast, and the seal's thin skull exploded and a spray of blood fell around and upon the boy. The boy swung again and again until he was awash with a delight of blood and he was a figure of bright red with the everlasting white behind him. It was as if the creature's very life had somehow leaped into the boy. And the three of us were silent in the witness of this wicked miracle. The boy danced about energetically, singing, while Edward McClintock skinned the seal. Then we returned, and the day was as cold as iron. None of us spoke but for the boy, who chatted gaily and sang. When I gave him his pills, he laughed and threw them into the North Atlantic Ocean.

I made it back to Rockefeller Center at 11:15 P.M. and raced backstage. The rundown was on the wall. Beside ANSWERING MACHINE SKETCH it read: CUT AFTER DRESS. I went to my dressing room, locked the door, and cried.

No one but the four of us ever knew of the journey. The boy made a complete recovery and was written up in several medical journals. Everyone agreed that his survival defied worldly explanation. The boy attained a small measure of fame and was even invited to Gracie Mansion, where he met the mayor himself. It was barely reported, a year later, when, while crossing Fifth Avenue, he was struck by a New York City bus and killed instantly.

I cannot find Norm's essence. It is a problem I've never encountered as a ghost, and I need to truly become him to finish the book. It has always been my great gift, the ability to find a person's essence. But Norm evades me. It must be because I hate him with such intensity. That simply cannot continue.

This will be the last book I ever ghostwrite, and I need it to be a fine book. You see, I have a secret, a splendid secret that has kept me going for many years. All the time I have been writing the lives of peripheral celebrities, I have been writing something else as well.

It is a novel. The tale of a brilliant painter, a master of surreal involution, whose work goes unrecognized by the New York art scene, and so our hero must make his living as a house painter. He becomes known as an excellent house painter, and he makes a fine living from his pedestrian work and nothing from his brash genius.

One day the great artist is commissioned to paint a house. The owner of the house will be gone for a month, and this gives the artist a notion. He decides he will use the house as his canvas. And so begins my novel, The House Painter.

And I have finally completed it. In front of me, on my desk, lies the manuscript for The House Painter, *beside the half-finished* Based on a True Story. *Like gold beside sand.*

26

TINY WHITE COFFIN

"It sure was tragic what happened to that boy, Norm," Adam Eget says, with a weighty expression that brings everything back to me like it was yesterday.

The boy had turned ten years old only a few days before the accident, and now he lay in Strickland's Funeral Home, in a tiny white coffin. When all the strangers had finished looking at him and sadly shaking their heads so that all present knew their feelings on the matter, his mother was left alone in the room with the tiny white coffin. Alone but for me.

I lingered behind, unseen, while the funeral director shooed the others into a room with a sad-faced pastor, who was preparing to speak. The mother stood and looked down into the tiny white coffin. Her posture, which had been rigid all morning, went slack at the shoulders and neck. Her hands remained clasped tightly in front of her.

The boy was wearing a navy-blue suit with a white shirt and a tie, but he still did not look like a man. I stayed quiet in the shadows so as not to disturb the moment.

After a time had passed, the funeral director opened the door and quietly let the mother know that her time was up. As she turned to leave, she looked one last time into the tiny white coffin, and then she did a strange thing, a thing I will never forget. She straightened the knot on the boy's tie and looked to make sure it was right. I took in a fast, jagged gulp of air and slunk into the next room before she noticed me.

There were cookies and an urn of coffee on a table in the other room. The cookies were awful. None of the cookies contained jelly in the middle, which are widely considered the best funeral home cookies. There were only dry shortbreads left. The coffee was black and there was no cream or milk, just packets of white-yellow powder. When I poured the powder into the Styrofoam cup of black, bitter coffee, it just sat in a pile on the top. When I mixed the powder in with a black plastic stick, the coffee turned gray like dishwater. It got me pretty steamed, and I'm sure the rest of the people who had gathered felt the same way.

We all went into the adjoining room and took our seats. The tiny white coffin had been placed in the front of the room and the sad-faced pastor was standing beside it. The sad-faced pastor told us how the boy had not been an ordinary boy. He had been very special. He had been a brother and a son and a grandson and even a great-grandson. I looked over and saw them sitting there, the young and the old and the older and the oldest. The sad-faced pastor told us that some things were very mysterious but that there was a meaning behind everything, even something as tragic as this. He then asked if anyone had anything they would like to say, and people came up one at a time to speak about the boy.

I decided to go up and speak too, since I had experience in public speaking. Of course, I wasn't about to do my stand-up. That would be ridiculous.

I pulled out the piece of paper with a speech I'd prepared, and then, when I was about to read it, I suddenly changed my mind. "Folks, I have in my hand here a speech I wrote that's full of big fancy words. But I'm not gonna read it." And I crumpled up my speech and threw it to the floor with contempt. "You don't want to hear a bunch of fancy words, many of them so fancy you wouldn't even understand them. Instead, I will speak from the heart. I have never done such a thing before, but I hear it can be quite effective.

"Ladies and gentlemen, bereaved relatives, youngsters who have lost a brother or a sister or a friend, the guy in the sad-faced-pastor costume, the lady sitting beside him—I figure it's his wife—and finally, of course, the guy hanging around at the door wearing a Carolina Panthers jacket who is clearly in the wrong room but has the grace to hang in here till the end: I thank you all for coming.

"I was proud to have known this boy and I was proud that his last wish in life was to see me do a sketch on the *Saturday Night Live* program. Although I cannot say I was all that surprised. I'm a very good sketch player. But this is not about me. I really shouldn't be making it about me, but this is the first time I have ever spoken from the heart, so I beg your indulgence. I feel this speech will really start to get good very soon."

But it didn't. And I realized something during the next twenty minutes as my speech moved from one inane anecdote to another, none of them having to do with the boy. What I realized then was that some guys are very good at speaking from the heart and some guys just are not. Doesn't mean one guy's better than the other, just different. So I was honest with the people.

"Ladies and gentlemen, I apologize for this speech. For the last five or six minutes I've been telling you about Gordie Howe, and I think we all know what an awful, awful mistake me speaking from the heart was. So, if I may ask your help, let's try to find that speech with the big, fancy words that I threw away some minutes ago. It's got to be around here somewhere."

"Here it is," a sweet old lady near the front said. "I read it and thought it was very good. Especially the part about how we can learn more from the children than they can learn from us."

"Oh, excellent. I'm glad you liked that part, because it's the surprise ending. So that's shot. I guess I'll have to just read it without the surprise ending. And there appears to be coffee spilled all over it."

"Oh, yes," the sweet old lady said. "I spilled coffee all over the darned thing."

"Okay, well, I can't make out any of the big fancy words now at all, but it's nobody's fault. I mean, in all fairness, part of it is my fault for crumpling it up and tossing it away so cavalierly. You know, I think 'cavalierly' may have been one of the big fancy words in my speech. Also, it's partly the sweet old lady's fault for spilling so much coffee on the paper that not a single word can be made out. But we're not here to place blame.

"I will say this about the young boy in the tiny white coffin. Despite the doctor's dire predictions, the boy was too tough, resolute, and courageous to let something as small as a deadly disease defeat him. No, the boy was made of stronger stuff than that and it took much more to defeat him. It took a three-ton municipal bus moving at forty miles per hour and driven by one Cecil Richard Anderson to defeat this boy."

I heard the deepest of sobs and looked down to see a man wearing some sort of bus driver's uniform being held up by two women.

"If you cry, sir, then cry with envy and not pity. For the boy is in the clouds and he is one with the clouds. It is we who are left who are reminded on this unacceptable day that life is swift and yet we are blind to its mighty splendor, which can be found in the simplest of things. Things like a walk in the park, a conversation with a good friend, a deep rich coffee leavened with half cream and half milk and served in a sturdy mug—one with some heft—and, with it, a delicious cookie that's white and has red jelly in the middle. Thank you for listening, and, due to the solemnity of the occasion, I would ask you to hold your applause."

From there, we all went to the graveyard. The day was bright and clean and the cool autumn air filled my lungs and made me feel healthy. A time passed and then the hearse showed up. The pallbearers were all big men and they carried the tiny white coffin as if it was very heavy, although it could not have weighed more than eighty or ninety pounds.

There was a small hole in the ground and some dirt beside it. We stood in a circle and the sad-faced pastor said some things in Latin and then we formed a line. The sun was directly overhead and made the tiny white coffin ever so bright, and I took a handful of dirt and flung it down on top. Then it was the next guy's turn.

Afterward, I walked back alone down a long blacktop road, and it was cold, and in the sky there were white clouds, and they all looked like white clouds and nothing else.

27

LEAVING LAS VEGAS

Gabe walks into the hotel room. He is much less surprised by my presence than Adam, and much less overcome by emotion as well. "Chickened out, huh, Norm? That'll cost me a pretty penny. I don't blame you, though."

"He didn't chicken out, Gabe. He's only alive by mistake."

Gabe looks relieved. "You won't get any more credit in Vegas, Norm. You're done until you pay off at least one hotel. The good news is these are businessmen. They aren't going to harm you; they'll be patient. But when they turn the debt over to collection agencies, those boys can make your life hell. And eventually you might be facing prison time. But you can cut a deal with the casinos and get on a monthly payment plan. These are reasonable men. They don't expect all the money back. They just want as much as they can get."

"Gabe, no disrespect, but I don't give a good Goddamn about all that. I'm looking to own a ranch in Montana, to be a god among men. I've been thinking, and I beat the Devil once; I can beat some

Vegas debt collectors. Hey, you wouldn't happen to have any more Dilaudid on you, would you?"

Gabe just looks at me.

"Like every man who's ever lived, Gabe, I spent my life searching for happiness. And after I'd lost it all and after I'd lain down in a bed and let go of my life, I arose from that bed and I envisioned happiness, real happiness. It involves living deep in Montana. It'll be expensive, and I know I'm in debt, but I can win the money. I know I can. I just need someone to stake me."

"How much?"

"I need a million dollars. I can win enough with that to pay off my debts and live a good and happy life."

"There's only one man who can help you with that problem. He used to be a bookie out of Galveston, but now he lives in a palace that overlooks the Salton Sea and he loans people money. Any amount of money."

I can't believe what I'm hearing. I've heard the stories about the fat man with the artificial hair for years, just like everybody else, but they always seemed like myths. And I know all about the Salton Sea. It is a geographic wonder, a real-life lake shimmering in the middle of the desert. And that's something even Las Vegas doesn't have. It was what was supposed to bring in tourists from everywhere, promising water and desert in the very same place. They began building resorts where guests could fish and water-ski and gamble and golf. At the time it seemed like a no-brainer and the investors flooded in, but in the end it was a bust and everyone left. But was it possible that one man stayed? A man with a mansion on the barren Salton Sea who lent out huge sums of money, but if anyone dared not repay him he exacted the ultimate price? It's true the fat man with the artificial hair had disappeared from Texas at about the same time that the men with money flocked to the Salton Sea. Was it possible he'd stayed behind, that he still believed? And now here was Gabe telling me it was true. "Gabe you're not telling me you believe the fat man with the artificial hair actually exists, are you?"

"Oh, he's real, all right. I know a guy who used to be a dealer at the Bellagio, and now he makes a thousand a day standing near the fat man with the artificial hair and holding a machine gun."

"If you say he's real, Gabe, then that's good enough for me. I'll go and find this man and I'll make my second deal with the Devil. Get the Challenger, Adam Eget. I'll be out in a minute."

When we are alone, Gabe gives me a serious look. "Keep your wits about you with the fat man with the artificial hair. If you offend him, he'll kill you and throw you into the sea. Where you're going now, there is no law. Someone will be guarding the mansion. In order to gain entry you must say, 'I am a desperate man, here to ask a favor.'"

"I'll remember that, Gabe, and I'll be careful."

Minutes later Adam Eget and I are moving so fast it feels like the Challenger is rolling down the steepest hill. I open the window and put my head out, with my mouth wide open, and my tongue licks up the wind. I am as happy as a dog.

"Adam Eget, we have very little money and it has to last until we reach the Salton Sea."

"Don't worry about it. If we need money, that's what liquor stores are for."

"No, that's not what they're for, Adam Eget. They're for selling liquor."

"No can do. One day at a time. Right?"

"Yeah, whatever. I'll need your gun."

Adam Eget looks hurt and I understand. I've never taken a man's gun from him, but Gabe had warned me about the dangerous place we are driving to, and I don't want Adam Eget deciding he's a man all of a sudden. He hands it over.

The Challenger screeches to a stop.

"Look, Norm, this has been fun, but please let me go home now. I miss the Comedy Store. I miss Pauly; I miss my job and being a boss. I've been thinking, and I did everything you asked of me when you told me about the plan at Whiskey Pete's."

"Well, things have changed since then, Adam Eget."

He looks at me steady. "Yes, things have changed. I've fallen in love and now I'm afraid of where we're going and what we're doing. Please, Norm, I've done everything you asked."

"I remember another time you were afraid for your life," I say, "and you were right to be afraid, but you are alive today because I saved you. Don't you remember the Night of the Gypsy? Perhaps it's been too many years. Perhaps you've forgotten."

"I remember, Norm, but I can't keep paying for that the rest of my life. What happens after all this is over?"

"Well, Adam Eget, then we will be all square, you and I. You will be a free man."

Adam Eget smiles.

"All you have to do until then is survive." His smile vanishes, and the Challenger resumes its journey as we move fast toward the Salton Sea.

28

WEEKEND UPDATE

"Hey, Norm, how'd you get Weekend Update?" I'm out of cigarettes so I pour a few grains of liquid morphine into a glass pipe. I use a torch lighter that sends an obelisk of hard blue fire to attack the glass and make the morphine sizzle and spit like bacon grease. My mind begins a crazy dance.

"Well, let me think, Adam Eget. Let me think."

There was only a week until my second season on *SNL* began. I was out of prison and had my immortal soul intact. Sarah had just announced she would be leaving the show. She said she could no longer live in New York, that she was being tormented day and night by some obsessive stalker. This caught me completely by surprise, as I had taken to hanging around Sarah's apartment, hiding in the bushes day and night, watching her come and go, and I had never seen any signs of a stalker. But she was gone now, and I had to turn my attention to my future at *SNL*. The problem was, Lorne still had no idea what to do

with me. The two of us had been partying pretty heavy for three days straight down at the Chelsea hotel, but we had been discussing a serious matter as well: What would my role on *SNL* be next season?

"You can't write," said Lorne. "You can't act or do characters. I simply don't know how we can use you." There was a lot of truth in what Lorne said, but it still hurt. I knew I could write, because I had been doing stand-up for years and had plenty of surefire bits that would make for dynamite sketches. And I knew I could appear in those sketches, because I'd performed those stand-up bits thousands of times, to wildly mixed reactions. I told Lorne as much.

He looked at me long and his eyes were tranquil and pale. "Norm, the thing is, you're not really suited for the show. You're more suited to touring the country, playing smaller and smaller clubs until you finally fizzle into oblivion and are given an unattended pauper's funeral," he said. There was a lot of truth in what Lorne said, but it still hurt.

Suddenly I saw a lightbulb go on over Lorne's head and his eyes brightened and I could tell he had an idea. But no such luck. It was just that Goddamned bare lightbulb that hung from the ceiling and kept going off and on all day.

Finally, as usual in creative matters, it was the drugs that thought up the idea. After Lorne had injected himself with a near-fatal dose of the opioid, his eyes rolled back in his head, then returned to where a fellow's eyes usually rest. "Let me ask you a question, Norm, and I want you to be completely honest with me."

"Of course I'll be honest, Lorne." *Fat chance.*

"If we let you sit down on a chair behind a desk and we stick giant cue cards two feet in front of your face, do you think you could read what is on those cue cards?"

"Of course, Lorne," I said, "and I won't let you down. I just have one question: Do I get to have a gun?"

I always asked this question every time someone had a plan for me, just in case they said yes. Like everyone else, Lorne said no.

"Let's celebrate by throwing the TV out the window," I suggested, but now Lorne looked concerned.

"I just remembered, Al Franken wants the Update spot, and he's been lobbying pretty hard for it. The truth is, he's much more qualified than you. He's been on the show since its inception, and there's nothing concerning politics or satire that Al is not on intimate terms with, whereas you're an illiterate nightclub comic." There was a lot of truth in what Lorne said, but it was really starting to get on my nerves.

"Look, Lorne, what if I was to tell you that if Al Franken were to step aside and allow me to host Update, I could make him a United States senator?"

"How could you possibly make that happen, Norm?"

"I know people."

I was telling the truth, but only technically. I did know people—more than two dozen, in fact—but none who could help make a civilian into a senator. It was a huge bluff, but Lorne bought it.

In an interesting sidebar, Al Franken, buoyed by the idea that the fix was in for him, ran for office in 2009 and became the junior senator representing Minnesota. He has not been heard from since.

"Hey, Lorne, I was thinking the best writer at *SNL,* Jim Downey, could be head writer of Update," I said as I tossed a double shot of morphine at his feet. "What do you say?"

Jim Downey *was* the best writer at *SNL*. He'd been there since the beginning and only left for a short spell to work on *Late Night with David Letterman*. He had helped usher into being two of the best and most original comedy shows of his generation. Not bad for a guy with a grade-one education. I knew that Downey's platinum writing credentials combined with my ability to read words off giant cue cards that the producers would place two feet in front of my face would be a potent mix.

"Well, the thing is, Norm, you are absolutely correct," said Lorne. "Jim is nonpareil."

Then he just looked at me. A long time passed—maybe forty-five minutes—until I finally said, "All right, all right. What's that word mean?"

"It means he is without parallel. He is the best writer we have. We use him to write all the political sketches."

"I have a better idea," I said. "He'll work for me. That way the jokes will all be surefire and I'll just have to read them."

"Sorry, Norm, Jim will write the political sketches. He's much too valuable to only be working on Update. When it comes to this show, Norm, you'll find I don't compromise. *SNL* always comes first."

"I'll give you three times as much morphine."

Lorne picked up his phone and dialed. "Jim, you're on Update from now on."

Thank God for Lorne Michaels and his hopeless addiction to liquid morphine.

29

THE UPDATE TEAM

The next person I got on the Weekend Update team was Lori Jo Hoekstra, whose talent was being wasted as a writers' assistant. She was always the funniest girl in the room and could keep up with the big boys, even Sandler, who loved her. Her taste in comedy was nonpareil, and I convinced her to be the producer of the segment.

I loved Ian Maxtone-Graham and wanted him exclusively on Update, but he was too important to the show and would have to split his time

between my work and the sketches. He served as a consultant along with Steve Lookner, who always submitted highly eccentric jokes.

From the outset, Lorne let me know that I could make Update

into anything I wanted it to be but that I would always have to deliver the jokes completely unarmed.

Lori Jo, Downey, and I discussed it. Before me, the Weekend Update staff had always been made up of just the host and one writer. But that was because the host would write jokes every week. I had a completely different style. I would write roughly one to two jokes every two years and spend most of my time practicing reading giant cue cards two feet in front of my face.

Lori Jo then suggested we hire outside writers so that Weekend Update would have a completely different flavor from the rest of *SNL*. She suggested Ross Abrash, a veteran comedy scribe who was the best in the business and the man who taught me what the word "scribe" means, and Frank Sebastiano, a UPS driver just like that fat guy on TV with the bitchy wife. Frank had been sending in two hundred jokes a week on brown paper bags, just trying to land a job. The jokes were so good that we hired him. The team was in place.

I'll never forget our first meeting. Jim Downey explained that Sandler had successfully remade *SNL* with his rockstar persona. He thought we should follow Sandler's lead and develop Weekend Update with a punk sensibility and cited the Clash as our muse. Everyone in the room agreed with Jim. Everyone but me.

"Listen here, Jim, one of the most important qualities for a performer to have is the ability to know his own limitations. I've never been a good singer. I'm the guy in front of the camera, and I'm gonna have to nix that one."

Jim explained that he meant the show should echo the ethos of punk rock, where everything but the essence of the music was stripped away. It really had nothing to do with singing. But I put my foot down and addressed the whole room. "I got two words for all of you, and if you want to keep your jobs you'll listen. NO SINGING!"

Jim just sighed, but I knew I'd been heard. Never once in my three years as Update anchor was a singing joke submitted.

Lori Jo agreed with Jim that the jokes should be stripped of any cleverness, play on words, or innuendo. Jokes should never elicit applause, Lori Jo insisted. A joke should catch people by surprise; it should never pander. Applause is voluntary, but laughter is involuntary. Lori Jo was sure smart and the whole room agreed, and I pretended to. But my mind was far away, on a meeting I had set up for later that afternoon with Wally Feresten, the cue-card guy. No offense to our team, but I knew that Wally and I were the key players.

Ian Maxtone-Graham spoke next. He said he loved the jokes that Frank Sebastiano was submitting, where the punchlines were preposterously blunt. I also loved those punchlines and said as much. The directness really made me laugh.

Ross Abrash wrote short, to-the-point jokes. There was never an ounce of fat in a joke written by Ross. Frank thought of new ways to tell jokes. ("Don't I know it!"; "Or so the Germans would have us believe"; "Note to self"; "Or as Ted Kennedy calls it . . . THURSDAY.") Together, they are the most copied joke writers of their generation.

"Exactly," said Downey. "That's what I was getting at when I said the segment should have a punk feel."

This time I smashed my hand down hard on the desk. "I SAID NO SINGING, GODDAMMIT!"

Jim sighed again. He was starting to realize that his dream of putting me on set with an electric guitar, singing and spitting on the audience, was not going to fly, so he decided to give up.

Steve Lookner had submitted an early joke. "Lyle Lovett and Julia Roberts are getting divorced. Insiders say the trouble began because he was Lyle Lovett and she was Julia Roberts."

I sure loved that joke. I'd never heard a joke where the premise and the punchline were so close.

"Exactly," said Downey. "That's what I was getting at when . . ." But I glowered at him and he cast his eyes down. If he wanted to listen to his Sex Pistols records, he could do it at home.

But Downey felt he should warn me that the type of comedy we were writing wasn't traditional, and I couldn't expect to get wall-to-wall laughs. This was avant-garde stuff. I didn't tell him at the time, but if not getting laughs was avant-garde, I'd been avant-garde week in and week out in stand-up clubs across the country.

Jim told me I had to think up a line to introduce the segment every week. The two best anchors were Dennis Miller, who opened the segment with "I'm Dennis Miller and what can I tell you," and Chevy Chase, who opened his with "I'm Chevy Chase and you're not."

I suggested, "I'm Norm Macdonald and here's a string of jokes." The group initially seemed amused but ultimately hated it.

I said, "I'm Norm Macdonald and this is the fake news."

No one liked this at all. The news was real, I was told. The news-cast itself was fake, but all the news within the segment was real. I disagreed vehemently.

"Are you telling me that the first parts of these jokes are things that really happened?"

"Yes," said Ross Abrash. "We always start with a real story from the news, not a fake one, and then we make up the last part, or the punchline, which is a comment on the first 'real' part, the setup."

"Well, I say you're a liar. You just make up the first part and then it's easy to think of a funny second part."

"No," Ross insisted. "I can assure you every setup we do comes from the real news. So saying 'This is the fake news' makes no sense and it makes you look like an idiot."

"Well, I guess we'll just have to agree to disagree," I said.

"No," said Ross. "I will not agree to disagree. I will only dis-agree."

I didn't know that was allowed, so I looked around the room. "Well, we've heard from Ross. Is anyone here in this room willing to agree to disagree with me?"

Not a single soul agreed to disagree with me. However, everyone was in solidarity when it came to simply and violently disagreeing with me.

Long after I left the segment, the term "fake news" became the ordinary way to describe what was done on *SNL* as well as *The Daily Show* and *The Colbert Report*. So who's the idiot now?

People often ask how many jokes I contributed to Weekend Update. The answer can be a whole bunch or one, depending on how you look at it. I pitched it during that first meeting. "David Hasselhoff is a major recording star in Germany, where his two shows, *Baywatch* and *Knight Rider*, are huge hits. Which all goes to prove my theory, Germans love David Hasselhoff." No one laughed.

Jim said, "You can do it, Norm, but non sequiturs have to be done often to have any chance to work."

"Okay, Professor," I sneered, "what's a non sequitur?"

"It's a joke that makes no sense. It's structured like a joke but has no content."

Jim was really starting to get on my nerves. That was no non sequitur. It was a real joke.

The meeting had held such promise, but it was turning bad quickly, and I sensed that two camps were forming: the camp I was in and the camp everyone else was in. I knew where I was needed. I quickly excused myself and went to meet with Wally Feresten to discuss the size of the cue cards.

The new incarnation of Weekend Update premiered in the fall of 1994 and was an instant hit. *The New York Times* hailed it "punk-rock comedy," which is what I had been intending for them to notice from the beginning. Frank and Ross wrote all day, every day, on Update, and by week's end they had generated maybe two thousand jokes. We'd cut it down to thirty for dress and to about a dozen for air. By that time the jokes would be bulletproof, exactly like one of those punk-rock songs.

We also filled the time with features, of course, and it was so fun to have Sandler do his Hanukkah song or Farley do anything at all, really. Later, guys like Jim Breuer and Colin Quinn came along and were perfect for features because they came from stand-up and knew how to perform directly into camera. And I got to sit right beside them and watch, and, when the camera wasn't on me, I could swig warm bourbon from a flask.

I knew Weekend Update was becoming popular, because my influence at the show began to build. I was a natural at reading cue cards that were held two feet from my face. I noticed that my power on the show was directly related to the size of the cue cards. I kept demanding larger and larger cue cards, until mine were over four times as big as any other cast member's. I even negotiated for Wally to get his own personal trainer, who would work with him during the week, since the weight of the giant cue cards was beginning to prove too much for him.

We were having a great time at Weekend Update until the grumbling began. I had heard things, but I just chalked it up to general grumbling. But it was not. It was grumbling that was specific to Weekend Update and specific to me.

But I never worried. Weekend Update was the funniest it had ever been, and when you are that funny, you can be sure that you will not be fired.

30

TOP 25 WEEKEND UPDATE JOKES OF ALL TIME

(in no particular order)

1. The Post Office announced today that it is going to issue a stamp commemorating prostitution in the United States. It's a ten-cent stamp, but if you want to lick it, it's a quarter.
—CHEVY CHASE

2. At the White House this week, President Clinton officially came out against same-sex marriages. What's more, the president said he's not too crazy about opposite-sex marriages, either.
—NORM MACDONALD

3. A new FBI study shows that, for the first time, Americans are more likely to be killed by a stranger than by a loved one or acquaintance. Their advice? Introduce yourself to as many people as possible.
—NORM MACDONALD

4. The American Academy of Pediatrics has announced its list of unsafe baby products. Topping the list this year is the really, really, really, really, really high chair.
—NORM MACDONALD

5. Dr. Jack Kevorkian was responsible for another death this week. This time it was a fifty-eight-year-old woman. She's the twenty-sixth of Dr. Kevorkian's patients to die since 1990. When are people going to realize this man is not a good doctor?
—NORM MACDONALD

6. The richest girl in the world, billionaire Athina Onassis, celebrated her tenth birthday this week. What's it like to be the richest girl in the world? Well, to give you some idea, at the party they had two cakes.
—NORM MACDONALD

7. A new hangover-free vodka is on the market. The ads claim that the eighty-proof vodka is so pure it's virtually headache-free. But, before you run out and buy it, remember, it causes massive anal bleeding.
—NORM MACDONALD

8. Julia Roberts told reporters this week that her marriage to Lyle Lovett has been over for some time. The key moment, she said, came when she realized that she was Julia Roberts and that he was Lyle Lovett.
—NORM MACDONALD

9. Well, the results are in, and once again Microsoft CEO Bill Gates is the richest man in America. Gates says he is grateful for his huge financial success, but it still makes him sad when he looks around and sees other people with any money whatsoever.
—NORM MACDONALD

10. This week in the O. J. Simpson trial, Johnnie Cochran delivered a spellbinding final summation. In a brilliant move, Cochran put on the knit cap prosecutors say Simpson wore the night of the

double murders—although O.J. may have hurt his case when he suddenly blurted out, "Hey, hey, careful with that. That's my lucky stabbing hat."
—NORM MACDONALD

11. In music news, number one on the college charts this week was Better than Ezra. And at number two: Ezra.
—NORM MACDONALD

12. According to a controversial new biography, Elizabeth Taylor likes her lovemaking loud, rough, and frequent. Coincidentally, that's also how she likes to eat.
—NORM MACDONALD

13. Well, it's official. Michael Jordan is leaving baseball to return to basketball. It is unclear whether the media will now refer to him by his old basketball nickname, "Air Jordan," or his more recent baseball nickname, "Señor Crappy."
—NORM MACDONALD

14. In Walnut Creek, California, anyone who turns in his gun can now get free therapy. And anyone who does not turn in his gun can get free anything.
—NORM MACDONALD

15. Earlier this week, Marlon Brando met with Jewish leaders to apologize for comments he made on *Larry King Live,* among them that "Hollywood is run by Jews." The Jewish leaders accepted the actor's apology and announced that Brando is now free to work again.
—NORM MACDONALD

16. At Virginia Commonwealth University, a professor is being sued after revelations that he spanked one of his students. It was the student's parents who became suspicious when they asked, "What kind of marks are you getting?" and she replied, "Big red ones on my ass."
—NORM MACDONALD

17. Yippee!!!!!!!! Jerry Rubin is dead. I'm sorry. That should read, "Yippie Jerry Rubin is dead." My apologies.
—Norm Macdonald

18. Former first lady Nancy Reagan reports that her husband has been relaxing at their ranch, riding horses and chopping wood. Sadly, eyewitnesses report that he was actually riding wood and chopping horses.
—Norm Macdonald

19. It was revealed this week that mass murderer Richard Speck, while serving a lifetime sentence in prison, was videotaped with hormone-induced breasts, snorting cocaine and having sex with a man. The film was apparently made with prison video equipment and a $300,000 grant from the National Endowment for the Arts.
—Norm Macdonald

20. Dr. James Watts, a neurosurgeon who performed the first frontal lobotomy, died this week in Washington. If you recall, a lobotomy involves drilling holes in the skull and then inserting and rotating a knife to destroy brain cells. What a genius. He'll be missed.
—Norm Macdonald

21. Officials in Disney World have ordered their ride the Extra-TERRORestrial to be shut down so they can make it even scarier. When the attraction reopens in two weeks, it will be exactly the same—but missing one bolt.
—Norm Macdonald

22. Last week, on his latest trial for assisted suicide, Dr. Jack Kevorkian startled a Michigan courtroom when he stood up and shouted, "This is a lynching!" Everyone turned to look, and, sure enough, he'd just lynched some old guy.
—Norm Macdonald

23. On Wednesday, World Chess champion Garry Kasparov tied Deep Blue, the IBM supercomputer that can examine 200 million

positions per second, in the fourth game of their six-game series. Earlier in the week, Kasparov admitted he made a "catastrophic blunder" in game two when he failed to force a draw by moving rook to e8, opting instead for a Caro-Kann defense that soon transposed into a Pribyl defense, which, after Deep Blue moved bishop to e7, gave it the advantage with its ninth position. With all due respect to Mr. Kasparov . . . what the hell were you thinking?

—Norm Macdonald

24. A French man, who calls himself "The Human Snake," was arrested this week after climbing up the side of a Manhattan high-rise. Yep, he climbed right up the side of a high-rise. Just like a snake!

—Norm Macdonald

25. In North Dakota this week, a hunter narrowly escaped death when a pocketknife in his breast pocket deflected a bullet shot by another hunter. Man, you know we have too many weapons in this country when people are getting shot in the knife.

—Norm Macdonald

31

THE FAT MAN WITH THE
ARTIFICIAL HAIR

A dam Eget slams on the brake and the car screeches to a stop in front of the Ski Inn. The parking lot is empty. At the top of a hill we can see the mansion that is home to the fat man with the artificial hair.

"Behold the Salton Sea, boys," the barkeep says, as he wipes a perfectly clean glass behind the bar. "Twenty years ago it seemed like a surefire bet, but look around and know that nothing is certain."

We look out the window, out at the uncertainty of it all. The town looks torn to hell, with the young meth heads stumbling around and giggling and scratching at itches that never go away, and the old men, rum-drunk, driving golf carts aimlessly through the rubble. No one goes near the beach. The sand beside the Salton Sea cannot be seen. This is because it is covered a foot deep in the broken skeletons of dead fish. And the stench is everywhere.

"What happened here, old man?" I ask. "What killed everything?"

"Salt."

"Listen, old man, you're not making any sense, and you're making Adam Eget nervous."

"I want to go home, Norm. I want to go to the Comedy Store and ask to get my job back."

"You see, boys, salt corrodes. It eats everything—steel, rock, the dreams of man. I've seen it with my own eyes, boys. Salt can even kill a sea and eat the fish that live there."

"But salt is what makes a sea."

"Too much salt," mutters the old man, and walks away. "Too much salt."

And so Adam Eget and I walk, ankle-deep in fish skeletons and sludge, up to the giant unfinished house on the hill, the house that contains my last hope in this cold, cold world. As I get close to the entrance I see the biggest red Cadillac I've ever seen. It's a beautiful thing how big it is, and I understand how a real fat guy would want a big car like this. And it's the brightest red, but even this expensive, beautiful car is not immune to the salt. There is disintegration along the edges, where the salt has eaten away at the steel. I hear a noise and there stands a boy who must be about ten years old, holding a big gun. "Whaddya here for?" the boy asks, and I carefully recite the line Gabe gave me.

"I am a desperate man, here to ask a favor."

The boy leads us through the house and into a large room.

The room is magnificent: red marble floors, oversize chairs with gold inlay on the mahogany arms, immaculately clean. There are three well-dressed goons, the type who like to punch you in the stomach, and they stand behind us. In front of us is a large table, where the fat man with the artificial hair is eating a meal.

"Sit down, boys." He invites us to the table with his meaty paw.

"We don't want to disturb your meal."

"Would you care to join me? It's tilapia. I caught it only an hour ago."

"But the bartender said that the fish were all dead. He said the salt ate them."

"He spoke the truth. The salt ate every type of fish but one." The fat man with the artificial hair picks up a piece of his fish with a fork. "Only the tilapia survived. It takes much more than salt to kill a creature like the tilapia fish," and the fat man with the artificial hair takes a salt shaker, twists off its top, and pours half of it in his mouth. I can hear the salt crunching like glass between his teeth. I look around and notice that there aren't any drinks on the table.

"How much you boys need?"

"He needs nothing, ever," I say, motioning to Adam Eget. "I need one million dollars, and I only need it for a week. The reason is—"

"No," he interrupts, without looking up. "It's none of my business. Carlos, get the man his million dollars. These are the terms: The first month is free. After that, I charge one percent per week."

"Hold on," I say. "That's ten thousand a week. That's pretty thick juice."

"Yeah," says Adam Eget as he stands up. "That's horseshit. No deal, fat man."

One of the goons quickly punches Adam Eget in the stomach and he falls to the floor.

"Did he just call me fat?" the fat man with the artificial hair asks, and the hurt in his voice surprises me. Adam Eget is doing his best to apologize, but he can't get a sentence out proper because he's still recovering from the massive blow. "Sorry if I was out of line . . . owwww . . . uggghhh . . . with that crack about . . ." That sort of thing. It'd be sad to watch if it wasn't so funny.

"So let me understand. You think that ten thousand a week is too much to pay me if you lose the million?"

"Yes," Adam Eget gasps from the floor. "I think that is too much."

"Let me ask you something, boys. Are you planning to lose this million dollars I am loaning you? Is this what I am hearing from you?"

"No, sir," I say. "No, not at all. I have a plan, sir, and it's not to lose. It's to win and to pay you back quickly, taking advantage of your generous first-month-free deal."

Carlos enters the room with a duffel bag, and I can tell by the way he walks that that duffel bag is heavy. A million dollars heavy.

"Sign this paper," says the fat man with the artificial hair. This catches me off guard, and I laugh. Here we are with two goons standing by Adam Eget, another with a red duffel bag full of money, and the fat man with the artificial hair is acting like we're in a legitimate bank doing legitimate business.

But I don't care; I'll sign anything. My name is as worthless as a bent penny, and if it helps me to scribble it on a piece of paper, no problem. But when I look down at the document on the table, I understand. It's a life-insurance policy he wants me to sign.

It will, upon my passing, pay two million dollars to my beneficiary. And across the table from me, smiling like a crocodile with salt-caked teeth and handing me a pen, sits my beneficiary.

"It came to me in a dream," he says.

I smile right back at him and sign the paper.

A piece of coal will never become a diamond, no matter how long you wait. That's the truth. But forget the truth. Coal is famous for becoming diamond.

Mr. Macdonald had a moment in the mid-'90s when he was a diamond, and I watched him on TV and thought he shone brilliantly and had facets. But it was a lie and we were all fooled. Mr. Macdonald was and is a sad, misshapen, crumbling chunk of the blackest coal.

Before I can walk once again in the sunshine of New York as an important author, before I am seen as the diamond I always have been, I must finish this damnable memoir. I must find Mr. Macdonald's essence. And to that end I must become him.

I have begun donning his preposterous wardrobe. Now when I look in the mirror, instead of seeing a fashionable New York gentleman, I see a costumed clown, a slovenly mess, each piece of clothing an advertisement for Macdonald's past success.

Twice when I have ventured out in the street with the costume, I have nearly been mistaken for him. I can see how people see me and search their memories for my name but are unable to bring it to their lips. A few times people have thought they went to school with me.

I have been poring through all the tapes he's given me, dozens of TV shows and movies I never realized he'd done, and each one is worse than the last. I'm captivated by the boxes of videotapes of Mr. Macdonald doing stand-up, stretching from thirty years ago to the present. The tapes are fascinating only in that they each contain the exact same stand-up material, word for word.

And finally I've been reviewing all the tape recordings of me interviewing him. On them, he often flares up with anger and shouts things like, "I'm giving you gold, Keane, gold, I tell you!" and I think, You have given me straw and a Rumpelstiltskinean task.

A few weeks ago, Mr. Macdonald called me from Las Vegas and told me a story of meeting Andy Griffith at an airport, and he insisted that the encounter be transcribed "word for word." I have never done such a thing. To let a celebrity's words, unvarnished, touch the page goes against every instinct I have as a ghostwriter. So after I hung up I phoned Julie; she's the boss.

To my surprise, Julie agreed wholeheartedly with Mr. Macdonald, telling me that what she is looking for is "authenticity." It must have been my imagination, but when she spoke I swore I could hear the oaf grunting like a swine in the background.

I do not consider myself a cruel man, but since it is out of my hands, I can't help but smile, knowing the reader will have to endure a small taste of what I have been force-fed a steady diet of for nearly a year now: a story by Norm Macdonald, word for word.

32

WORD FOR WORD

It's true what they say. Never meet your heroes. It turns out they're all a bunch of fucking assholes. They're probably the reason you turned into such a fucking asshole—because they were your heroes and you spent all your time trying to be like them. Lemme tell you a story from my life so you can understand what I mean.

It was a day like any other. *Except* Ben Matlock was standing really close to me. But, besides that, it was a day like any other. *Yeah, right.* Like every day Ben Matlock is standing really close to me. That's a laugh.

I was at the airport because I had to take a plane because I had to go do stand-up in Portland, Oregon. I'm really good at stand-up. Then I look over into the bookstore and who do I see? You're never gonna believe it. It was Ben Matlock. I shit you not. And he was standing there, reading one of those big books. You know the kind. Usually you can't even understand their stupid titles, and when you try to read them you get one word in and get really sleepy. And it's so stupid to try anyway, because if the stupid book is any good they'll make a TV movie out of it and then you can watch that instead. They'll probably get an actor like that guy from that one episode of *Mannix* to be in it. What the fuck is that guy's stupid name anyway? The guy who was in that one episode of *Mannix*.

Now, you must remember this happened a long time ago, back when Ben Matlock was still alive.

Literally nobody but me had spotted Ben Matlock, and I didn't want to blow his cover, but I sure did want to meet him. Who knows, maybe we would become friends and I would introduce him to my buddies by saying, "You know who this guy is? This is old Ben Matlock himself! He never lost a case. Hey, Snake, you should hire this guy next time you get in trouble. He'll keep you out of the joint. Just stop making your stupid face and show some respect and get the man some cheese."

The problem was, I hadn't even met Ben Matlock yet and I knew at any time old Ben might hear his plane was ready to go, and then I'd be fucked. I shit you not.

I needed a plan, but fast. I looked at a table with some books on it. I searched for a title like *How to Come Up with a Plan, but Fast* or *The Art of Fast-Planning*. But no. Nothing. Just a bunch of fucking shit.

I grabbed an *Archie* comic from the rack and began to read it as I snuck up beside Ben Matlock. It was that one where Jughead gets a job at Pop's Chocklit Shoppe, and the gang can't figure out why he took it, because Jughead is such a useless bum who's always mooching off his friends, but it turns out that Jughead just took the job 'cause he knew they'd let him wear one of those oversize chef's hats and he could use the hat to steal hamburgers. That Jughead is a dirty, thieving sonofabitch, but he sure does make me laugh.

When I was right beside Ben Matlock, I threw the *Archie* comic away and grabbed the biggest, thickest book I could find and turned to a random page. Then I loudly said, "What the fuck? I certainly didn't see that shit coming." Ben Matlock turned his back to me.

I kept talking but way louder this time.

"I don't know about you, fellow, but I love books. And the bigger and heavier, the better."

Matlock turned and looked right at me. I almost fucking shit my pants. I shit you not.

He's like, "I must say it's refreshing to see a younger man who appreciates literature."

And so then I'm like, "Oh, yeah, I love all that shit. I'm a comedian by trade, but mostly I like reading big long books with titles you can't understand, and of course I like TV shows, especially ones about lawyers and . . . heeeeeeeeeeeeeeeeeeeeeeeeey, I just realized who you are! Why, you're my favorite TV lawyer of all . . ." And that's when my mouth got real dry and I had no words and I realized I'd been tricked.

It wasn't Ben Matlock at all. It was just some old man. He didn't even look like Ben Matlock.

I'd just spent over two minutes talking to some old man. Who the fuck would ever do that?

There's not a day goes by that I don't think about that stupid old man and how much I hate his fucking guts.

33

WAY OUTTA LINE: THE MAKING OF *DIRTY WORK*

Many times, young people will approach me to ask me how to make it in show business, and I always offer the same foolproof advice. Just remember three little words: "Meet Adam Sandler."

The rest pretty much takes care of itself. Sandler had vouched for me to be on *SNL*. In the summer break he put me in his first film, *Billy Madison*, and then he told Robert Simonds, who produced *Billy Madison*, "You should give Normie a movie." And that was that. I went from being a low-paid road comic to starring in my own film due to one guy's help. I've never thanked Adam for doing all that for me or told him how lost I'd be without his generosity. And I never will either. That's because I'm a self-made man.

So I had an offer to do a movie but no ideas. That's when Frank came to the rescue. One night while we were working late on Update, Frank came up with a concept. The movie would be about a guy who is good at getting revenge, so he and his buddy open a revenge-for-hire business. Later in the film, it turns out his buddy is actually his brother. SPOILER ALERT!!!!!

We brought on a third writer, Fred Wolf, who worked with us at *SNL* and had plenty of motion-picture experience.

Robert Simonds told us that the next task was to select a director. This turned out to be a problem. I wanted Frank to direct *Dirty Work*. He knew the script better than anybody and had studied film at NYU. But the biggest reason I wanted Frank was that I already knew him. If we didn't hire Frank, I would have to meet some new guy and learn his name and pretend-laugh at all his jokes and ask him if his parents were still alive and listen as the guy told me that they both died last week, days apart from each other. Then I would have to buy the guy an expensive watch. I really hated meeting new guys.

So I got Robert Simonds on the phone. "Robert, I think we need to talk about a director."

"I got just the guy," said Robert.

"Is it Frank?"

"No, it's Bob Saget."

"What are you, nuts?"

"Let me ask you this, Norm: What comes to mind when you think of Bob Saget?"

"I don't know. A bunch of shit, I guess."

"Norm, he's more than *Full House* and *America's Funniest Home Videos*. Did you know that he's already directed a film and won a Student Academy Award?"

"What?"

"That's right. It was a film school documentary called *Through Adam's Eyes*. It was about his seven-year-old nephew who underwent facial reconstruction surgery. I watched it. Very moving stuff."

"Well, thanks for the wonderful news, Robert. And now, if you'll excuse me, I have to run."

"What's the hurry, Norm?"

"I have to buy Bob Saget an expensive watch."

When Frank, Fred, and I were writing *Dirty Work*, we had actors in mind for each part. I don't have the imagination necessary to create a man out of nothing, so we decided to go the opposite route: We wrote the movie by choosing our dream cast first and then writing characters based on them. We wanted Don Rickles. We got him. We wanted Chevy. We got him. We wanted Jack Warden. We got him. We wanted Sandler. We got him. We wanted Chris Farley. We got him. We wanted Bill Murray. We're still waiting to hear back.

Our only problem was that we had written the script as a buddy comedy, and we hadn't yet cast the buddy. When it came to comedy films, Frank and Fred were experts. They told me that since I was a skinny guy, my buddy should be a fat guy. I got real mad and decided I needed to remind them who was boss.

"That's a bunch of horseshit. What about Laurel and Hardy? They were both skinny and they were really funny."

Turns out I was wrong on that one. So I continued, as my face grew red with anger.

"And what about Abbott and Costello, or Ma and Pa Kettle, or Burt Reynolds and Dom DeLuise, or Jackie Gleason and Art Carney, or Belushi and Aykroyd?"

It seemed that every example I came up with not only hurt my argument but bolstered theirs. But I saw a way out.

"Well, it takes a big man to admit he's wrong, and I admit I'm wrong, so I'm a big man. A big, big man. What about you two, are you wrong?"

Frank answered. "No, Norm, Fred and I are right."

"That's what I thought. Which makes you both very small men. And I feel sorry for you."

We looked at every fat guy in Hollywood, but nobody seemed to work for the role, and we were beginning to panic. Then one night, three days before we were supposed to fly to Toronto, I happened to turn the TV on and, for the first time ever, I saw an episode of

MADtv. An actor named Artie Lange was talking straight to camera, not in character, and he was hilarious. What impressed me the most was that he wasn't relying on fat-man tricks; he had a melancholy about him that reminded me of Belushi. I knew instantly that he was the guy for the part, so I phoned Robert Simonds and told him about Artie. But it was a big part and he informed me that an audition was necessary, so Artie met with Bob Saget and me.

Artie's reading was perfect and I knew we had our man. When he left, Saget and I phoned Robert Simonds, and Robert said, "If he works for you guys, let's do it."

But an hour later, Robert Simonds called back. "Bad news. The guy's got a big coke problem."

"So what?" I said. I had six grams of morphine rushing through me.

"Listen, Robert, you know as well as anybody that it's drugs that make a guy funny," I said.

"Of course, Norm, but this guy got caught. He went to jail. It's public record. That's why he's back in New Jersey, out of the business."

"Goddamn!" I said.

"Look, we can still make it work," Robert said, "but we have to be sure he stays clean the entire time he's in Canada. Can you promise me that?"

"No," I said.

It was such fun to be back in Canada, my true home strong and free. I was born in the Great White North and I remain to this day a Canadian citizen and I will till the day I die. I'll tell you why. Canada is the country that shaped me, that taught me right from wrong, that turned me from a boy to a man. Also, that American citizenship test is way, way too hard. Trust me, I've tried it quite a few times. But no more. You know the old saying: Fool me once, shame on you; fool me twice, shame on me; fool me thrice, shame on Adam Eget, pretending to be me and failing even worse; fool me four times, shame on the guy behind the desk at the Immigration and Naturalization office, who said he would see what he could do for a hundred clams and then said that he couldn't do a damn thing but kept the hundred clams anyway; fool me five times, shame on the filthy homeless bum who could rattle off all the presidents in less than a minute but then the moment I gave him twenty dollars to do the test in my stead took off running down the street with a whoop and a holler; fool me six times, shame on me again, for threatening to burn down the federal building in New York City if I wasn't given citizenship immediately. There would be no seventh time. Nobody ever accused this old country boy of being stupid. But it turned out to be all for the best, anyway. I've finally come to my senses. I was born a Canadian and I'll die a Canadian and I will forever be proud to count myself a citizen of Canada, the fourteenth-greatest country in the world.

A month after our first phone call, Bob Saget and I walked down the longest street in the world, Yonge Street in Toronto. People recognized Saget everywhere we went and would say, "Hey, you're Bob Saget!" and Saget would turn to them and say, "Thank you," as if it was a compliment. It was hot and crowded and dirty on the longest street in the world.

Yonge Street runs near a hundred twenty miles from north to south. You can visit the Hockey Hall of Fame there or have a donut and a cup of coffee at Tim Hortons, and the runaway kids are on every corner, selling love to the Americans, who go up there to make movies cheap. And in the summer of '97, the kids that nobody misses were missing and there was a bad man on the loose. And it wasn't Saget. And it wasn't me. And it wasn't Adam Eget either, I don't care what anybody says.

Adam Eget had done things, sure, but they weren't bad things. They were the things that young men do when they need money. Breaking and entering, stealing cars, selling those pills you're supposed to take when your ankle hurts real bad, smuggling cigarettes across the border, and jerking off punks under the Queensboro

Bridge for fifteen dollars a man. Those kinda things. But nobody ever got hurt meeting Adam Eget. Still, Saget and I decided we would keep Adam Eget outta sight so the Ontario Provincial Police wouldn't be sniffing around the movie set. If they saw a way to blame this whole Yonge Street unpleasantness on a young American boy, that would be just dandy with the Canadian John Law. Just dandy.

34

MR. WARMTH

They say you should never meet your heroes, and I guess they're right, okay. At least that was the experience I had with one of the actors on *Dirty Work*. He didn't disappoint me as an actor. He was brilliant in the film. No, this man disappointed me in a deeper way. He disappointed me as a human being. I'm speaking about Don Rickles.

Now, I was a huge fan of Mr. Rickles and was thrilled at the prospect of finally meeting him. I guess I knew just about every word from *Toy Story*, where he played Mr. Potato Head. I also loved him in *Toy Story 2*, where he reprised his role as Mr. Potato Head. And I would be negligent if I didn't mention how great he was in *Toy Story 3*, where he played Mr. Potato Head.

But I also knew him from *The Tonight Show Starring Johnny Carson*, where he was a frequent guest. When he visited Johnny, I must say, in all candor, I never found him funny. Johnny, a true gentleman, always kindly introduced Don as Mr. Warmth, and then Don would come out and, let's just say, not live up to this nickname.

Don would immediately begin in on poor Johnny, being boorish and, yes, I'll say it, in some cases downright insulting. Now, don't get me wrong. I'm no fan of phony-baloneys. I like a man who is direct; I like a man who is honest and plainspoken. But there is a big difference between frankness and insults designed to hurt people. And somewhere along the way, I think, Don lost sight of that difference.

I approached him the first day, in the makeup trailer, and introduced myself as I sat down. "I just want to tell you, Mr. Rickles, that I feel so honored that you would agree to be in the film, and I thank you from the bottom of my heart, sir."

He shook my hand. "That's very nice, Norm. By the way, I spoke to the home. Your room will be ready Tuesday."

The trailer erupted in laughter, and I felt rage deep in my soul. I caught sight of myself in the mirror and saw that my face was beet red. I wasn't on any waiting list for any type of home, as Mr. Rickles was clearly suggesting. But I swallowed my anger. I was determined to find the real man through my own kindness and love.

"Mr. Rickles, I would be honored if I could take you out to one of Toronto's finest restaurants and buy you dinner tonight."

"I have a better idea, Norm. Why don't you go to a shed in the desert with a rake and go BRAAAAAAP!!!!!!" This awful classless burping noise got the cheap laugh I'm sure Mr. Rickles is used to, but not from me. I could feel myself begin to shake with rage as everyone laughed at me. But I held it together.

"Well, maybe a raincheck, then, sir. If there's anything you need while you're here, just let me know." I could see I'd finally gotten through to him, because he gave a wide smile and put his arm around me. "Actually, Norm, there is one thing you could do for me, if it's not too much trouble, and I'd be forever grateful."

I was so happy to finally reach the real Don Rickles, and I said, "Anything, sir; what would you like?"

"Well, Norm, I'd like you to get a monkey and an organ grinder and run around the room going, 'I lost my sock, I lost my sock.'"

And Mr. Rickles then pranced around the makeup trailer, doing a grotesque pantomime of me searching for a missing sock.

Now the laughter rose to a volume I'd never heard, but I knew it was not genuine laughter; it was the type of laughter that springs from nervousness and embarrassment. I felt burning tears run down my cheeks, and I fled the makeup trailer. I took a nice long walk, trying to compose myself. I think it was the comment about losing my sock and then running around telling everyone that hurt the most. Some things are just beyond the pale. I thought of Johnny Carson and how he was able to take this sort of abuse from Don, time after time, while the whole nation watched. It was a testament to Carson's great security as a performer. Any other host would have had him ejected from the studio.

When I felt whole again, I returned to the makeup trailer and decided to give Mr. Rickles a few words he'd probably never heard but certainly needed to. I stormed in without knocking.

"Now, listen, Mr. Rickles, we are going to be working together in this film and I do not want any hard feelings, so I have a few things to say. I think that much of what you do is frankly insulting; it is completely uncalled for."

"That's great, Norm; now, why don't you take a train to Wyoming and milk a Clydesdale." This was again followed by a long period of embarrassed laughter from everyone present. It stung like a wasp, but I kept my dignity and with a quavering voice told him once again how happy I was to have him on the project.

I don't regret telling Don Rickles what so many were afraid to. I guess, looking back, my only hope is that one day Don will remember my words, reflect on his life, and make some really meaningful changes in the way he chooses to treat people, especially strangers who pay good money to see him in nightclubs and theaters.

35

THE SHOOT

The shooting of the film was a blast, but getting to work with such experienced and talented movie actors proved to be a double-edged sword. Now, I understand that all swords have two edges, so let me save some time by taking that back and just saying that getting to work with such experienced and talented movie stars was a sword. By watching these actors work, I could study them and steal many of their acting tricks. But I always felt they had no respect for me as the star of the film. Often I would catch them gathered together as I performed a scene, and I could not ignore their withering glances. They looked at me the way real vampires look at Count Chocula.

But that was not to be the worst of it. Not by a long shot. I had brought Adam Eget to Toronto to assist me on the film. Once again I must emphasize with all the vigor at my command that Adam Eget never once *assisted* me.

On the tenth night in Toronto, Bob Saget woke me in the middle of the night. There was a problem with one of the cameras from the

previous day's shoot, and we would have to redo a scene before the sun came up. So I stumbled out of bed and phoned Adam Eget, but there was no answer. I knocked on his hotel room door. No answer. So I took a cab to the set.

We reshot the scene, then I rushed back to get two hours of shut-eye. When I woke up, there was Adam Eget with a muffin and a coffee.

"How'd you sleep, boss?"

"Not well. Where the hell were you last night?"

"I was in my room."

"I phoned you a hundred times; you didn't pick up."

"Oh, yeah, that phone is broke," he said, blushing.

"I knocked on your door for ten minutes."

"Yeah, I think that door might be broke too."

"Where the hell is my paper?"

"What paper?"

"The *Toronto Star* you bring me every day with my muffin and coffee."

"Oh, the guy at the front desk said they went out of business."

"That's absurd. Go get me my *Toronto Star*, Adam Eget."

He returned ten minutes later with a newspaper with the front page torn off. "What's going on?"

"The guy said you could have this one for free since it has no front page."

"Tell me the truth, Adam Eget."

"A young man's body was found in a ravine last night. He was a teenage runaway, just like the rest. I thought you might suspect me."

"Did you have anything to do with this?"

"No, of course not, boss."

"Well, where were you last night, then?"

"I couldn't sleep, so I did what I always do when I have insomnia. I went out and found a ravine to relax in."

"A ravine?"

"Yeah, a ravine."

"Was it the ravine where the teenager's body was discovered?"

"Oh, no. Jeez, I could see why you'd be suspicious if it was the same ravine. No, this kid was found two ravines over."

"Well, who the hell goes to a ravine to relax?"

"Not me anymore, that's for sure. This whole thing's giving me the willies."

"Well, I told everybody that you weren't in your room last night. The police will be all over the set, and if anybody tells the cops that . . ."

"I'm scared, Norm. Should I buy a gun?"

"A gun? No. That would be the worst thing you could do. If the police talk to you, you have to tell them you couldn't sleep last night so you went for a walk down Yonge Street." I paused for a moment. "You wouldn't kill a string of runaway teenagers, would you?"

"Norm, you know I couldn't harm a fly."

"Right, but what about a teenager?"

"Never."

"Okay, buddy, let's get to work."

That morning's scene was one where Artie and I got in a huge bar fight. It was very physical and involved a lot of stuntmen. I didn't want the stuntmen to roll after they landed, 'cause I always thought that looked fake in movies. I wanted them to stop abruptly when they hit the cement, which was much more painful for the stuntmen. Frank, Fred, Saget, and I were going through the choreography of the thing when I saw two police officers in the corner, speaking with Adam Eget. "Hold on, guys," I said. "My stupid friend needs my help."

By the time I'd made it to Adam Eget, he was already cuffed and being led away. "Hold on, hold on, there must be some mistake."

"We're just going to the station and having a little talk, that's all," said one of the cops.

Well, that settled it. There was not much I could do but get back to work and forget about this. Chris Farley showed up and we all sat down to have some breakfast. Twenty minutes later I got a phone call. Adam Eget had made a full confession to the murder of fourteen teenagers.

I phoned Robert Simonds at once.

"Robert, you're not going to like what I'm going to tell you." I told him the whole affair.

"Norm, I'm gonna be straight with you, because I've been in this business a long time. If the star of a movie has a personal assistant who, during the production of that movie, butchers over a dozen teenagers, that's gonna hurt at the box office."

"Well, he had nothing to do with it, Robert." A production assistant suddenly ran from the other side of the room and whispered in my ear. "Oh, well, this is not good news, Robert. I've just been told the media has dubbed this affair 'the *Dirty Work* Murders.' Now, that doesn't seem fair at all."

"We might have to pull the plug on this, Norm." And he hung up.

At the police station, I muscled my way through the crush of reporters to get inside. When I saw Adam Eget, he was sitting in a small interrogation room with a big smile on his face and two pies on the table before him. One of them was nearly finished.

"Hey, Adam Eget, how are you holding up?"

"Fine. We can leave soon. I just want to finish this second pie. The first was cherry, but I saved my favorite for last, strawberry rhubarb." He whispered the last part as if it was a secret.

"Why do you think we can leave after you finish eating?"

"Because, that's the deal. The policeman asked me what I wanted and I said I wanted to go home. And he asked if I wanted anything else, and I said, 'Two fresh pies.' And he said that if I signed a paper, then I could get my pies and then go home."

"That paper you signed, Adam Eget, that was a confession that said you killed fourteen people."

"But, Norm, you know I couldn't murder a fly."

I wasn't sure what to do. "We'll get you the best court-appointed attorney in the whole city."

Back on location, the arrest of Adam Eget had cast gloom across the set. I hadn't told anyone about it, but word gets out in this media-soaked age. Every day, the actors would have to dodge the press on their way to work. And the questions invariably had nothing to do with the film. The media, as usual, was interested in one thing and one thing only. I decided to hold a press conference so these buzzards would finally leave us alone.

"Ladies and gentlemen of the press," I said. "I appreciate that your city has endured a nightmare of vicious murder that began two days after we started pre-production on our movie, *Dirty Work,* an MGM film that will make its theatrical debut next summer. The motion picture has very good buzz about it and I would hate if this unpleasantness somehow hurt that. Of course, a film is not as important as a young person's precious life. I understand that my personal assistant, Adam Eget, has been dragged into this unfortunate affair by signing a full confession to all of the killings. But, trust me, Adam Eget couldn't murder a fly. He just has a sweet tooth, that's all, and since when did loving a fresh-baked pie become a crime? Also, I would implore you not to continue to refer to these killings as 'the *Dirty Work* Murders.' I know that's a lot to ask, so, in order to help, I have come up with a list of names for these murders that I honestly feel are much better. I will be handing the list out to you after I finish speaking, along with a Dairy Queen gift certificate for one hundred dollars. I will now take questions, and I hope some of them will be about the film."

None of them were.

I finished the presser and returned to the set. We were shooting a great scene that day. It had been Fred Wolf's idea. In the scene, Artie and I break into a mansion and hide rotting fish inside, thinking it will be unbearable for the people who live there. While we are busy hiding dead fish, the owners come home, and Artie and I hide in the next room. But the owner is there to complete a multimillion-dollar drug deal, which goes horribly wrong, leading to a shoot-out, a chainsaw murder, and finally a grenade that kills everybody. But all that activity is heard offscreen, while the camera stays on Artie and me, frozen, holding our ridiculous fish, our expressions never changing. I wanted the shot to be completely static—for Artie and me to be totally still—and I wanted the scene to last for one minute. We initially had trouble filming the scene because, after cameras were trained on our faces, Saget started saying things like "Okay, now you hear gunshots," and "Uh-oh, a guy has a machine gun," and "Now a guy just pulled out a chainsaw. . . ." And on it went; it was very distracting. But the idea was that Artie and I would have one blank expression of terror for the whole scene, and it was tough to hold that with Saget blabbing on and on. I finally told Bob to just say, "Action," and a minute later say, "Cut." The take went well and we were happy, but it didn't last for long. Wouldn't you know it, moments after we finished the scene, a production assistant came up and silently handed me that day's *Toronto Star*. DIRTY WORK KILLER ADMITS TO 60 MORE CRIMES IN THE TORONTO AREA. It was beginning to look like Adam Eget was more trouble than he was worth. After the day's shooting, I went back to visit him.

He was weeping softly and shoveling pie into his mouth.

"Adam Eget," I said, "I'll get you pie if you want pie. You must stop signing things."

"I'm afraid, Norm. Do they have the chair up here in Canada?"

"No, they don't have the death penalty."

This news put a big smile on his face and he ate his pie faster.

"But we're going to get you off on this, Adam Eget, don't worry."

And so we toiled on the movie, but what should have been a joyous time was instead full of grief, as funny scenes were trumped by coroner's inquests, and *Dirty Work*, which had been conceived as a buddy film, became the nickname of the most notorious crime in Canadian history. I couldn't wait for the whole thing to be over so I could get back to the United States and as far from Adam Eget as possible. Even though I knew he was innocent, I was tired of the whole affair and, when it came down to it, with Adam Eget's small brain, life on the inside would be the same for him as life on the outside. I just hoped none of this would hurt the movie or my career.

Then one day something wonderful happened. Jack Warden approached me as I ate lunch. "Did you read the paper today?" he asked, beaming.

"No, Jack, why?" I asked.

"I'll tell you why, kid. A runaway teenager was found dead this morning in a ravine."

"No way! That's the greatest thing I've ever heard!"

"Isn't it?" said Jack. "That clears your boy Adam Eget."

"It sure does. And it means they won't shut down the film."

Saget came running in, deliriously happy, clutching a newspaper. "They found a murdered teenage boy in a ravine this morning. Isn't it fantastic?"

Farley entered, dancing a jig, and bellowed, "Guess what, everybody? A monster is still on the loose and no teenager in Toronto is safe. Yahoooooooo!"

It seemed everybody was getting the good news at the same time. And that day the mood of the movie set changed for good. It's funny how something as small as the news of a teenager being slaughtered and tossed in a ravine can be enough to lift the spirits of an entire set full of important Hollywood people.

The next day Adam Eget was released from prison, and the press stopped using the term "the *Dirty Work* Murders" and instead called them "the Very Bad Guy Murders," which was one of my original suggestions. We returned to work on the film, and from that point on it was the best summer I ever had.*

It turned out that my worries about Bob Saget were unfounded. He did a great job directing the film, and there isn't a performance in the whole movie that isn't funny. When the film finally opened, the critics were split. Some hated it, while others hated its guts. But it didn't matter to the public. On its opening weekend, *Dirty Work* grossed 250 million dollars.

---

* In 2006, a drifter from Baffin Island named Albert H. Codfish was arrested for "the Very Bad Guy Murders." He made a full confession. In 2008, the city council of Toronto passed a law commanding that every ravine in the metro area be manned by police officers night and day. Since then, in the city of Toronto, Ontario, Canada, no one has killed anyone.

36

TORN APART

The duffel bag full of cash is in the trunk of the idling Challenger, and we sit by the Salton Sea, ready to go. But where can we go? Vegas is out of the question. As soon as word leaks that I took a powder after losing a million at four different casinos, nobody on the Strip will take my action. I could always turn to online betting, but trying to collect a massive win from an off-shore account is a hopeless endeavor. I'd have to get lucky twice, once to win and another to collect. So that leaves only one option: Atlantic City. The problem is that Atlantic City doesn't take sports bets, so I'll have to win at the tables. The other problem with Atlantic City is that it's three thousand miles away and our time is precious. The fat man with the artificial hair has the meter running.

We fill the Challenger with gasoline at a run-down station off Highway 111 and get the hell out of this apocalyptic wasteland. We're driving east down Highway 8. The white Challenger is moving me toward my fate at the rate of 70 miles every hour. This will be the last of it. Win or lose, my twenty-year gambling spree will be over. *It has all been such a waste.* It's not the wasted money that gets me, because money comes and goes. It's the time. And with that realization I feel a profound sadness, as I remember all the wagers, all the adrenaline, the bad bets, the lucky wins, and all of it for nothing. I know, in this moment, that my fever has broken and that I will never again feel joy or despair at the roll of a die or the turn of a card. I will feel nothing. Now I'm free. And the profound sadness I'd felt only a moment before melts away, and the cessation of pain produces joy, so I begin to laugh, which makes Adam Eget laugh, which makes me laugh harder and him laugh harder yet, and now the Challenger is filled with hysteria. I have not been this happy since I was a little boy.

The gamble is gone.

The laughter goes on for a long time and only our exhaustion ends it. When long laughter ends, something serious is always said. Adam Eget says it.

"Norm, I was thinking, we could always turn around and go back and give the fat man with the artificial hair his money back. You could cut some kind of deal with the Vegas casinos; Gabe said they do that. You could work. You could go on the road and you could pay off your debt little by little. I would go with you. I'll help you get out of this."

He is right, of course. That is the smart play. The chance that I can make the one million sitting in the duffel bag into the three million I need to pay my debts and buy my ranch is remote. I consider what Adam Eget says, and a few times I nearly ask him to make a U-turn back to sanity. Then, somewhere on the road, somewhere in the darkness, I remember something. Atlantic City is where all of this began. Atlantic City is the reason Adam Eget must stay with me and not go home to where he wants to be. Of course this must end in Atlantic City. How can I lose?

The gamble is back.

A moment passes and I can suddenly see Atlantic City ahead in all its shabby splendor. Snow begins to fall, just as it fell nearly twenty years ago. I look at Adam Eget, and Adam Eget looks back at me for a long time. This turns out to be a huge mistake, as the white Challenger finds a patch of ice and slips from the highway and is torn apart by tree after tree. Adam Eget is thrown clear, but I am not. I see total black and then bright white light.

37

THE BRIGHT WHITE LIGHT

I t is as white as salt. I am walking on white sand. I can feel it between my toes, but when I look down I have no toes, or legs, or
body either. So instead I have to imagine what I looked like when
I had those things, and when I finally see myself I am wearing jeans
and a plaid shirt and I am young. I am not walking as much as being
led by my imaginary feet, and I am approaching the source of the
whiteness, which is as brilliant as diamonds and as soft as wool. And
in the whiteness I see figures.

"STAY WITH ME." I hear Adam Eget's voice from far away.

My aunt Barbara is there with Uncle Bert—he was the beloved
town doctor who delivered babies and accepted chickens as payment. He was a saint. They are standing beside a Christmas tree,
under which is the Louisville Slugger I received when I was six years
old. I see my first dog, Tracker, and drool drips off his big red tongue.
And there is Anna, whom I last saw when she was eighteen and I
loved her and we said we would be together forever. They beckon
me toward them with outstretched hands and I approach.

"STAY WITH ME."

But then a thought occurs to me, one that had never occurred to me in my whole life: that there is still unfinished work back in the real world. The fact of the matter is that I hadn't really done any work whatsoever back in the real world and now I am starting to regret it. What if one of these jokers in this white world all of a sudden asks me what I accomplished when I was alive and I have to tell him, "Nothing, I just never got around to it"? That wouldn't sound too good. I could just make up stuff, the way I did down in the real world, but I'm scared that, here, they would know I was lying. So I decide I can't stay. I'll go back, do some sort of grand work, maybe back at *SNL,* and then return to these people and brag about my fine and finished work forevermore to all who will listen. And so I bid the dear departed adieu and turn on my imaginary heel to leave.

"STAY WITH ME."

My uncle Bert smiles tenderly. "Wouldn't you like to go with me to the deepest lake you can imagine, where we can spend the day trying to fool a trout with a bit of flying feather? Or perhaps we'll take Tracker and try to rustle up a grouse. How does that sound, boy?"

"STAY WITH ME."

Well, it sounds pretty good, all right, but that's not what clinches it. What clinches it is Anna. I look at her and notice she is still eighteen and that I'm eighteen too. I remember our promise, so many years ago, that we would be together for all of time and our love would never die. But Anna was too gentle for the world and its cruel ways and she jumped from a bridge on her eighteenth birthday. And so I decide right there that I will stay. I will stay here and hold Anna's hand and we will walk together into the white, white light.

As I approach my loved ones, I say, "Hey, where's Uncle Basil, anyway, and Aunt Ida? Why, they were the most pious people I ever knew."

They all fall silent, except for Tracker, who starts in with a low growl, and I remember with a start that Tracker had to be put down after he killed that infant girl. And hadn't there been talk around town that Uncle Bert, the beloved country doctor, may have spent years injecting patients with polio and not the polio vaccine? And then I remember the house fire that took the lives of Anna's parents a year before her suicide. That unsolved house fire. And this makes me recall that Uncle Bert never mentioned water in that deep lake of his. And that's when I begin to hear the gnashing of teeth.

"STAY WITH ME!"

The whole bunch sets upon me and I scrabble backward, but it is no use. Anna is first to grab me, and she doesn't look young anymore; she looks dead. She grabs me by the hair, and Tracker dives toward my groin with his teeth bared. I move quickly to my left to avoid the hound's terrible bite, but I lose my footing and I'm surrounded by a circle of the damned. Some guy who is a dead ringer for Old Jack appears, and he smiles and then raises up that Louisville Slugger and brings it straight down, quickly and violently and directly at my heart.

I open my eyes and cough deep-red blood onto the white snow. Adam Eget is directly above me, his sweat pouring onto me as he brings his entire weight down through the palms of his hands to the center of my chest.

38

FIRED FROM UPDATE

"**N**orm, I told you this when I first spoke to you four years ago. It is imperative that you always have an exit strategy."

"But I don't wanna leave, Lorne. I'm happy where I am, sitting behind a desk reading from cue cards that are placed two feet in front of my face. I like working ten minutes a week, and I don't plan on going anywhere. Besides, I just finished shooting a film. Don't you want a big-time movie star reading the news?"

"Well, when you leave is not your decision, Norm."

"It's not?" It had never occurred to me that it wouldn't be my decision when I left the show. I had long ago decided that I would spend my entire career on *SNL* but had forgotten to inform Lorne about it. But if it wasn't my decision, then whose could it be?

"Are you telling me you don't like me, Lorne?"

"It's out of my hands, Norm. But I know Don wants to talk to you."

Don was Don Ohlmeyer, the head of all the entertainment shown on NBC. I'd never met him, but I knew he lived in Los Angeles and had an office there and brown hair.

"Why does he want me out, Lorne?"

"He won't tell me. Don believes that it's cowardly to deliver such news over the phone, so we're flying you out to Los Angeles. The plane leaves within the hour."

Next thing I knew, I was sitting in the great man's office.

"Norm, are you aware that I am very good friends with O. J. Simpson?"

"Oh, yes, sir, I am, and I know I have been pretty hard on him on Update. I apologize for that. I guess where the blame really lies is in my institutionalized racism."

"Oh, no, Norm, you don't understand. I never had a problem with the jokes. I loved them. I just noticed that about six months ago you stopped doing them. You never bring O.J. up at all anymore."

"Well, Don, that's because a jury of his peers found Mr. Simpson not guilty of all the charges filed against him. He's as innocent as you or me. If I was to mention O.J. at all on the telecast, it would be to deliver a profound and heartfelt apology for the cruel, racist remarks I made in my self-appointed role as judge, jury, and executioner."

"Norm, I've known O.J. for many years. He's a close friend. I visited him in prison every Monday morning, and you know how I'd greet him, Norm?"

"No, sir, I don't."

"I'd give him the business about this whole double-murder thing. Lay a couple of zingers on him from your Update segment. Boy, old O.J. would see red, I'm here to tell you. And the more steamed he got, the funnier it struck me."

"Well, it's nice to know you liked the jokes, sir."

"Well, there's the rub, son," said Don. "Ever since he's been acquitted, he and I golf over at Brentwood. We have a standing tee time every Monday at six A.M. Problem is, you've decided to stop doing jokes about him and I don't have anything to zing him with. Do you follow?"

"Sir, I hope you're not asking me to do what I think you are."

"If you want to save your job, Norm, get back to the O.J. jokes. You promise me that and I promise that you can have Update as long as you like."

"I don't think I could do that, sir. What about the jury system and fair play and all that?"

"Oh, c'mon, Norm, O.J. can take a joke. They're all meant in good fun. And I'm just a guy who works hard trying to make the TV viewers happy. Heck, the only kicks I get are when I can give my friend O. J. Simpson the business. Now, you wouldn't want to take that away from me, would you?"

"I'll have to think about it, sir."

But there wasn't a lot to think about. I flew back to New York and talked with Lori Jo, Downey, Frank, and Ross. We all agreed that what we had done to O.J. had been unconscionable. We had been mostly fueled by my lifelong institutionalized racism. Now that we'd woken up to that fact, to continue to make O.J. jokes while the real killers were at large was out of the question. And for what? So Don Ohlmeyer could get under his pal's skin at the Brentwood Country Club?

The only thing O. J. Simpson was guilty of was being the best running back in history. And while O. J. Simpson had proven himself to be the greatest rusher, I had proven myself to be the greatest rusher to judgment.

39

A DEBT INCURRED

I t happened the night I was fired from Update. I wasn't a compulsive gambler at the time, but within twenty-four hours I would be. I was feeling low after the program ended. While my friends waved at the studio audience and held up little pictures for people they knew were watching TV, Adam Eget and I raced down the New Jersey Turnpike, and it was black except for the stars in the sky and the eyes of the deer on the highway side. We hit Atlantic City at dawn. The casinos sat square in the center of the squalid streets, streets lined with boarded-up houses and stores with signs that read WE PAY CASH FOR GOLD FILLINGS and the dangerous poor with nothing to lose but their lousy, stinking, hopeless lives and nothing of value but the gold in their teeth. It was Sunday morning, and instead of a church Adam Eget and I were checking in to the Devil's house: The Tropicana Casino and Resort.

Gambling addiction is a disease, for sure, but it's the only disease that can make you very wealthy. Osteoarthritis ain't gonna make you dime one, friend. Just ask my aunt Gertrude. However, gambling addiction can also be a fatal disease. When a doctor tells you that you have six months to live, he's making an educated guess. When the fat man with the artificial hair tells you the same, he's letting you know a fast truth you can mark on a calendar. The only cure for it is cash, and they won't likely be holding any telethons for you. My friend Sid Youngers once said, "I've been very lucky with gambling. I've never won," and anybody with a gambling

problem understands that statement, all right. First time I was ever in a casino I was unlucky. I won, and I won big.

Back in those days Adam Eget drank, and he drank like a man. I don't know if he drank to remember or to forget, but, boy, could he drink. We ordered two shots of Wild Turkey 101 and told the bartender to leave the bottle be. And the bartender was rightly impressed. After we'd emptied the bottle, I hit the blackjack tables to bet my five dollars a hand, and Adam Eget wandered onto the boardwalk, stumbling and muttering and telling anybody who would listen how he deserved much more than he had. The next time I saw him, my three-hundred-dollar bankroll was down to one eighty.

"I met a gypsy," Adam Eget slurred.

"What?" I asked, eager to get my next bet down.

"I went to one of those fortune-tellers to get my palm read."

"I never figured you for one to believe in that horseshit."

"I did it as a lark, as a gag. But here's the thing. The old woman, the gypsy, she looked at my palm and her face darkened and she looked up at me with her black gypsy eyes, and my laugh got caught in my throat and I wished I'd never had the idea for the lark, for the gag. She told me I was gonna die, Norm. She told me I was gonna die tonight."

"Well, then, how come I booked two rooms?" I asked, and I laughed hard at my fine joke and so did the dealer, but Adam Eget did not. He continued with a straight face: "She wants one hundred dollars, and she'll give me a packet with some powder in it that I'm supposed to put under my pillow. If I do that, I won't die tonight."

"Well, can't you see she's making the whole thing up, Adam Eget? You'll be fine."

"That's what I thought. But when I went to bed I couldn't sleep. Every time I closed my eyes I saw the old gypsy's face and heard her words. I'm scared, Norm. You have to lend me a hundred dollars."

"I'm losing money at this blackjack table, Adam Eget, and I won't indulge your silly superstitions. If you want a hundred dollars, why don't you just jerk off seven punks?"

"I told you about that in confidence," he said.

"You did?"

"Yes, of course."

"Oh, I thought everybody knew you jerked off punks underneath the Queensboro Bridge for fifteen dollars a man."

"Don't say that anymore."

"Okay, sorry. I didn't know you told me in confidence."

"Don't you remember I was crying when I told you?"

"Sure I do, but I thought that's what you fellows do."

"What do you mean, 'you fellows'? I'm not gay," he said.

I stood corrected.

"I'll give you twelve dollars for one," said the dealer, "but not a penny more."

Adam Eget looked at the dealer, and he appeared hurt. "Look, fellow, I don't do that stuff anymore. That was before and this is now. And now I'm Norm's assistant. That's my job. And I need an advance. One hundred dollars' advance."

As I was talking to Adam Eget, I'd lost another thirty-five dollars, and I got angry. "Get away from me. It's still early, and if I end up winning I'll give you a hundred dollars so you can pay the old gypsy. But until then get out of here."

With that, Adam Eget slunk away, whimpering. It put me in mind of a hyena.

I changed tables and had a run of good luck. My bankroll was up to two fifty now and I was approaching even. This went on and on and time passed, as it always does since it knows no other way. One minute I was up and the next I was down. When I only had a hundred-dollar chip left, I took a break and walked around the casino. As I passed a craps table, a patron recognized me.

"Hey, you're somebody, aren't you?" a man holding two dice said.

"Sure I am," I said. "I'm Norm Macdonald and I'm on the TV."

This got everybody very excited, because they were just a bunch of nobodies who had TVs but were never on them. They insisted I play craps with them, but the problem was I'd never played the game and didn't know any of the rules. But I couldn't let these nobodies know that. "Sure I'll play, and I'll win too!" The whole table of nobodies cheered, which made me feel good. The truth was that, deep down, I felt like I was a nobody too, just like them.

Behind the craps table stood the pit boss, a handsome man dressed in the most beautiful suit of clothes I'd ever seen. He was looking the picture of style and class, but I got the feeling that he was a dangerous man and his beautiful clothes were designed to hide that fact, the way a shiny new violin case can conceal a machine gun.

If you don't know the game of craps, here's how it works. As long as the fellow rolling the dice doesn't roll a seven, you stay alive. And when they hit your number, you win. And you can have as many as six different numbers. The minimum at the table was twenty-five dollars, so I put down my hundred-dollar chip to get change, but the man behind the table placed it on the pass line and I was too embarrassed to correct him. It was all the money I had left.

An Asian player rolled five or six times and a six came up, and the pit boss gave me one hundred twenty dollars. "Press?" the man behind the table said. I didn't want to look like a know-nothing, so I said, "What do you think?" as if the answer was self-evident. I use that line a lot when I don't know what's going on. The man smiled, and now I had two hundred twenty down. From there on in, every one of my wins was automatically pressed. He only asked me that first time. Within twenty minutes I had money on every number on the board, and within forty minutes I had a lot of money on every number. This Asian player, he didn't seem to know how to roll a seven, and my chip denominations had climbed from the original five-dollar chip to a thousand-dollar chip, and finally, at about the hour mark, I was playing with the maximum five-thousand-dollar chip. The funny thing is, the five-dollar chip was the very same size as the five-thousand-dollar chip. Probably cost the same to make. But it was worth a thousand times more.

I was winning big time now. I began to feel an extraordinary transformation taking place deep within me, one that mirrored my chip's transformation, for I felt myself double in value and then redouble and press to the maximum. I was the same exact size physically, and yet I was worth much more, a thousand times more, and that lingering suspicion that I might be a nobody was long gone. The Asian player rolled for twenty more minutes, and finally he rolled a seven and the run was over. Everyone cheered and I had a hundred eighteen thousand dollars in chips. I colored up, threw a fifty-dollar tip on the table, and left in perfect calm and elation, big as God inside, blessed on this Sunday in the unlikeliest of places.

I walked onto the boardwalk, my heart and pockets full. The people around me all looked small, and I knew that I was once like them but now I was different—same on the outside maybe, but a thousand times as bright, a thousand times as powerful, a thousand times what they were. I saw the blackjack dealer I had first sat with and lost one hundred twenty dollars to. "Remember me?" I asked.

"Sure I remember you," the dealer said, and I noticed he was zipping up his trousers. "Your friend's over there, and he's twelve dollars richer." I walked over and saw Adam Eget and he was on a bench, weeping. When he saw me he fell to the ground and clutched at my ankles.

"Norm, please, I need you to punch me in the face," he said.

"Don't be ashamed, Adam Eget," I said. "A man must do what he can to make a living in this world. And sometimes life can be a hard, hard coin."

"No, I need you to punch me in the face so I can sell my gold fillings. It is nearly midnight and I am very afraid."

"Don't worry," I laughed. "I am blessed by God Himself this Sabbath, and you will not die tonight." And as I said that, I carefully counted out eighty-eight dollars' worth of chips and tossed them down on the boardwalk, and Adam Eget got on his hands and knees as they clattered around, searching them all out in the dark, and then he kissed my feet and ran to find the old gypsy.

I awoke with a plan. I hesitate to call it my own plan, since it did not exist when I fell asleep the previous evening. It was as if another man had spent months conniving and creating the plan and then had come to me as I slept and staged it whole in my mind.

For three weeks now, an enfeebling depression has fastened me to my bed. The House Painter *has been rejected by every publishing house in the city. I'd expected a bidding war, but I hadn't even received an opening salvo. When the rejection letters first began appearing in my mailbox, I was amused and I felt sorry for each poor chap who had passed on my masterpiece and would certainly one day lose his job over the decision. But as the rejection letters kept coming, despondency fell upon me. Was it possible that the years of transcribing lame anecdotes of marginal celebrities had atrophied my skills to the point where my real writing was unpublishable? My first anxiety came with the silence of Julie Grau. I thought perhaps she hadn't received the manuscript, so I put another in the mail and, a week later, sat in shock over a cup of coffee while I read an unsigned form letter from Random House. I rang Julie up.*

"Oh, Terence, how lovely of you to call."

"What's wrong with it?"

"Your novel? Well, to tell you the truth, I simply haven't had the time to read it. I just got back from ..."

"What's wrong with it?" A long silence followed.

"There's nothing wrong with it, Terence. It is really quite charming. Have you considered self-publishing?"

A much longer silence followed.

"Terence, how is the Norm Macdonald book coming along?"

I threw the phone through my window.

And that is what put me in my bed and kept me there, eating Häagen-Dazs and Kit Kats, Milky Ways and Twix, drinking Mexican Cokes, watching Bewitched, and falling asleep, and waking up, and falling asleep again. But this morning I awoke with the plan; I bounced to the floor, showered, shaved, and put on my best shirt. I carefully read my novel as if I had never written it. I had to be sure, absolutely sure. I have just finished the last line and I am as certain as ever. It is pitch-perfect.

And now I put a fresh page in the old Underwood and begin composing another work. Although the task of writing has always been a laborious process for me, there is no tedium this time. The words come easy, and very fast. Perhaps I have found a genre perfectly suited to my skills: the suicide note.

FLIPPING COINS

've been convalescing in this suite in the Tropicana for about a week now. I got the same one I got almost twenty years ago, for the luck. Most of my purple flesh has turned yellow, and that means I'll be able to move soon. I relax in my big hotel bed as I reflect on my life and career. This turns out to be a huge mistake. Anxiety begins to crawl across my motionless body like a spider. So, instead, I begin to reflect on the life and career of Adam Sandler. This calms me.

Adam Eget comes busting into my room.

"Hey, great news. Sammi is flying out. She'll be here tomorrow morning."

I hate when people say they have good news and then they don't.

"Oh, yes. Sammi, the lady who is definitely not a dude. So, she's flying all the way out here?"

"Yeah, we're pretty serious, Norm. I think I'm in love with her. I'm thinking of asking her to move in to my place."

"But you don't even have a place."

"Well, yeah. Don't tell Sammi, though."

Our trip has cost Adam Eget his apartment and his job. But it will all soon be over and he'll be a ranch hand in Montana, and the head ranch hand too. I haven't told him yet, but I plan on buying him a hat. A cowboy hat.

Adam Eget is very excited that Sammi is on her way. He grabs a handful of nickels from my video-keno nickel jar and runs from the room like a boy in search of gumballs.

The next morning I sit in the coffee shop and chat with the two of them. I remind them that the first time they met was in a Las Vegas coffee shop. They find this to be the most hilarious coincidence, and Sammi giggles and Adam Eget hugs her and beams pride.

"Tell me, Sammi," I say, "what do you do for a living?"

"I'm a plumber."

"Isn't she the cutest?" Adam Eget asks. "Listen, honey, you want to come watch me play video keno? I'm up eighty-five cents."

"Oh my God, video keno is my favorite game," Sammi says. "What are the chances?"

I agree the chances are a billion to one. Maybe these two are made for each other after all. The happy couple leave, arm in arm, and I finally have some peace and quiet to consider my betting strategy.

Here's the thing about the tables. In order to have the best chance at winning, you should take your entire bankroll and bet it all on a hand of blackjack or a round of craps. The thinking is that the house edge becomes more certain the more hands you play. The less you play, the less you're against it. Simple as that. I would have bet the whole million in a heartbeat if it was permitted.

New Jersey law allows you to count cards, but the casinos continually reshuffle the deck, so it renders card-counting worthless. I would have to wager the maximum five thousand dollars at all times and simply hope to get lucky. Before my first session, I go to the restroom and splash cold water on my face. The sight of Sammi, with her neon-pink lipstick and drum-tight skirt, has unsettled me. I am beginning to feel sorry for my friend. This romance will not end well.

I'm two hours in now. I began my night with craps and I've recently switched over to blackjack, running a good shoe, playing five thousand dollars a hand, three hands at once, and I am up somewhere near two hundred thousand. Suddenly I hear a huge commotion and the dealer says, "Somebody hit it big over by the bar. You ever play the slots?"

"Oh, all the time. I mean, that's the smart play," I say with unconcealed disdain. I'd heard that siren so often over the years, the hoots and the hollers. It's the sound of dumb luck, and it always made me angry as hell. Where is the justice? Some idiot risks nothing, plays a low-stakes slot machine, and is awarded a fortune, while I risk huge money with no chance at a jackpot.

A moment later I see Adam Eget and the woman he is in love with running toward me, laughing and clutching a ticket.

"I didn't even have to pick any numbers, Norm. As soon as I put my nickel in, there was all this ringing and it seemed to last forever, and then this ticket came out."

He shows me the video-keno ticket, and I can't breathe. It reads 2.6 million dollars. I am saved. I sit at a table betting five thousand dollars a hand, but I am saved by a squid with a nickel. I am holding 1.2 million and Adam Eget holds 2.6. I do the math quickly. We owe two million and we hold 3.8. That's a profit of 1.8 million smackeroos. The journey is over. It all started on a black, silent stage at The World Famous Comedy Store, and now it ends in the same bright casino where I saved Adam Eget from the spell of an evil gypsy. And now the self-same Adam Eget stands before me. He has paid off his debt; he has saved my life. And then I hear her voice: "Let's go cash it in, honey bear! We're rich, we're rich!"

"Sammi," I say, "could I have a moment with my friend?"

She looks at me with suspicion and I can see she's mulling it over, trying to find the smart play. Finally she says, "Sure thing, Mac," and gives Adam Eget a kiss, before grudgingly walking a dozen feet away.

"Wow," I say. "I knew you could do it. I believed in you and you didn't let me down. Best investment I ever made."

"What do you mean, Norm?"

"Nothing, just that it was my nickel that you used to win the ticket. Therefore it's my ticket."

"Oh, dang," he says, and sighs deeply. "I thought I had won something really big. For the first time in my life, I felt like a winner."

"Oh, no, not at all. You're still not a winner," I say, and I snatch the ticket from him.

I return to playing blackjack, but every moment or so my hand touches the magic ticket in my shirt pocket. I try to act natural as I play five-dollar hands the way I used to nearly twenty years ago, but the corner of my eye remains closely on Adam Eget and Sammi. His shoulders are slouched and his movements are slow, but Sammi is animated and her hands are gesticulating wildly. Suddenly, Sammi strikes him across the face, and she follows it up with what looks like a long and angry speech, a speech she punctuates by frequently jabbing her finger hard into his chest. When she is done she points at me, then slams the heel of her hand into his back, and he stumbles forward and slinks over to where I sit. His right cheek has a big red paw print on it.

"Hey, Norm, I was thinking about it, and we never really had any deal worked out and, after all, it was me who won the jackpot, and I have a whole bunch of witnesses."

"Now, you listen to me, Adam Eget. When you talk about witnesses, you're talking about a court of law, and if that's where you want to take this, fine. But who do you think a jury would side with—you or a guy who's been on the TV?"

He looks at me and then at Sammi, and I can tell he doesn't want to go back to Sammi without the ticket. So I have to continue. "Put yourself in the jurors' minds. Do they believe the guy who has starred in two motion pictures and is a close personal friend of Adam Sandler or the guy who jerked off punks underneath the Queensboro Bridge for fifteen dollars a man?"

Adam Eget looks at me plaintively. "You promised you'd never bring that up. Please never tell Sammi that. She's very old-fashioned. She wouldn't understand."

"Of course I would never bring that up. But in a court of law, under oath made with my hand upon the Holy Bible, I'd have no choice. And they'd probably televise the trial. I'm just glad your mom doesn't have a TV."

Sweat appears in a mist on Adam Eget's forehead, and he gulps for air. "But she does have a TV, Norm. She has two!"

"Don't worry, I'll figure this out. You just go and tell Sammi that I want to take you guys to the best restaurant in town tonight, where we will discuss this like gentlemen—I mean two gentlemen and a lady. But for now you tell her to go to the spa and relax. And then you come back here and I will have a big surprise for you."

I place my chips in front of me but once again look at Adam Eget and his true love from my eye's corner. She still appears very angry but finally relents and leaves. Adam Eget returns. "So, what's the big surprise?"

I take him over to the cage and toss a black chip to the teller. "Give this man two thousand nickels," I say.

Adam Eget is dumbstruck. "No way—two thousand?"

"That's right, and what's more, from now on I want us to be partners in this video keno. You clearly have a feel for the game. Next time you hit the jackpot, you keep all the money, then the next time I keep all the money, and so on. Whaddya say? Partners?"

I've never seen him so happy, and he sticks out his big baseball mitt of a hand and we shake on it. I turn back to the teller and toss her another black chip. "Another two thousand nickels for my friend. I believe in this man." The teller is very annoyed, but Adam Eget is deeply moved. Now all I have to worry about is Sammi.

That evening at dinner, Sammi makes her intentions clear. The ticket is to be returned to Adam Eget or the police will be involved. Adam Eget looks from Sammi to me and back again, like a dog afraid of getting beat. I have to say something, so I do.

"I'll tell you what. I'm a fair man. How about we split it down the middle? We each get 1.3 million dollars. Think about it, Sammi. That's big money. That'll buy a lot of women's clothing."

"Yeah," Adam Eget says, "and imagine the ring we can get." He turns to me. "Norm, I want you to be the first to know. I have asked Sammi to marry me, and she has said yes and made me the happiest man in the world."

"Gross," I say.

Sammi stands up, all six foot four of her. "Excuse me? What did you just say?"

"No, I was just saying these french fries are gross. I'll be having a word with the chef about this. But first let me congratulate you two kids. I'm sure you'll be so happy together. Now, about this ticket: Don't you think we'd be best off just splitting the money? If we take this to a courthouse, they'll have all kinds of questions about our pasts and our work history and our gender."

Sammi studies me for some time, and I begin to worry that she'll take her chances in court. Finally she speaks. "Okay, this is how it's going to go down. We cash the ticket together in front of everybody, and just so there's no funny business, I'm phoning a friend of mine, a lawyer who lives in Philly. She'll be here by tomorrow."

"That sounds fine, Sammi," I say. "Come on, Adam Eget. Let's you and me get some rest," and I get up to go, but she stops me.

"There's one thing left to discuss," she says. "Who holds the ticket?"

"I'll hold the ticket!" I say.

"No," says Sammi. "Not you. Adam is the only one we both trust. He is gonna place the ticket in the safe in your room and use a combination that only he knows. When my lawyer friend shows up, we'll open the safe and go to the cashier."

We all go back to my room, where we make a big production of putting the ticket into the safe, which takes much longer than it should, because Adam Eget can't think of a "good number." When he finally settles on one, Sammi grabs him by the ear and leaves the room. "Until tomorrow morning, you stay with me." She thinks she's got me, so I play along, looking mighty disappointed that I can't be with the man with the combo, but I have other ideas.

Then I return to the blackjack tables. I hit a run of some bad luck, but I'm betting five dollars a hand, so it's actually very good luck. Besides, I'm only there to kill a little time, and as soon as I feel I'm not being watched I cash out and go find Andre, my host. When you lose as much as I do gambling, you can get a lot. And besides, the room is in my name and my name only. It's a fairly simple request. I just tell Andre I've run out of money and forgotten the combination to my safe. Andre summons an engineer and the three of us proceed to my room.

When we walk in, I see Adam Eget on the floor. His hands and feet are bound with rope, and he has duct tape on his mouth. I tear it off.

"The wedding's off, Norm."

"What?"

"I'm not marrying the only woman I ever loved. And you want to know why? Well, I'll tell you. Because she's not a woman, that's why. She's a man. She showed me right to my face. Very close to my face."

"Don't worry. You're better off."

"But I loved her, Norm. I loved her more than anything in life, and she broke my heart and took the ticket."

"I know it hurts now, Adam Eget, and I know it feels like the pain will never go away, but the funny thing about love is that— THE TICKET? THE TICKET! WHAT DO YOU MEAN, THE TICKET?!?!!!!"

"I gave her the combination. She told me that if I didn't, she would beat me up. I don't care about the ticket, Norm. I loved her and now she's gone forever. I don't want to go on living."

Problem is, I do.

I get down to the floor as fast as I can and get to the cashier's cage and ask if she's been seen. I'm told she was here, had cashed the ticket, filled out all the necessary paperwork, and was gone. I can file a police report, I am told, but people like Sammi are hard to find, and I don't have a whole lot of time.

I think that if I go back to my room I might kill Adam Eget, so instead I return to the blackjack tables. I need to win. I am alone at the table and playing all the spots, five thousand dollars each. I am playing smart and patient.

It takes me nearly six hours before I bust. "Better luck next time, sir."

The familiar gloom of losing everything falls upon me and I wander the floor, alone and lost. As I pass the cashier's cage, I hear a ruckus and look over and see a man in a loud argument with the cashier. I move in close and, when I do, I recognize the man.

It is Adam Eget, reeking of cheap gin and trying to cash in his five-year chip.

41

AFTER THE FALL

We sit in the Tropicana coffee shop not drinking coffee. I drink warm whiskey and Adam Eget drinks cold, cold gin. Now that all hope is gone, a deep relief has taken its place, and I allow myself to enjoy it before the despair sets in. Adam Eget tells me that he has just gotten off the phone with the Comedy Store and that Pauly Shore said he could return as manager. He tells me that he is going to quit drinking again and this time for good. He says maybe he will find a girl, a real girl, and settle down.

"Sure," I say. "Everything will work out just fine." But the truth is, I have less hope for Adam Eget than I do for myself.

My phone rings and the voice on the other end sounds familiar. "Tough last hand, Norm. But you gotta split eights, right? Even against an ace."

"Yeah, that's what the book says." I'm starting to get scared.

"Ten thousand a week, Norm. First month's free."

Well, that did it fast. The face came to me immediately, with its crocodile teeth and doornail eyes. The voice on the line was the fat man with the artificial hair. I down my drink and yell loudly for another.

"He already knows, Adam Eget. God knows how, but he already knows. I gotta get ten thousand and I've got less than three weeks."

"Oh, that guy. Yeah. Well, I don't want to say I told you so, but I always felt those terms were a mite steep. And what if, by some miracle, you manage to scrounge together ten thousand dollars—what's that buy you? Another seven days of life, that's all." Now that Adam Eget was a stinking drunk again, he was making a lot more sense.

"But I have no other choice; this is the bed I made, and it's the bed I must now lie in."

But Adam Eget is calm. "What if I were to tell you that you could pay him the whole million, all at once, and you just have to do one thing?"

"What is it?" I say. "What do I have to do?"

Adam Eget relaxes his body backward against the booth, swallows a mouthful of cold, cold gin, and speaks.

"Finish the book."

I like having no phone and a phone-shaped hole in the window. The apartment can get pretty windy at night, but it doesn't bother me. Nothing has bothered me since the day I awoke with the plan. It is just so perfectly rational.

As you can see, I am not a romantic. No great writer is. But the public is a different story. A posthumous work can be highly appealing. A book that took twenty years to write, which was then summarily and callously rejected, causing its author to take his own life—now, that is downright irresistible. Add to this that the manuscript in question is top-notch literature and we have the makings of a tragedy. By ending my life, I will live forever.

The only decision left to make is the manner of the self-murder. Pills seem like the simplest out, but there is something about the rope that is just so classic. We'll see.

I will finish this note and then finish myself.

42

A FANCY NAME FOR A FILTHY THING

Atlantic City hurt us all, and that included the white Challenger. While I convalesced in a hospital the car was being made whole in a body shop. Now it is hidden in an alley behind Keane's apartment, and we are bounding up the fire escape and busting through Keane's door. As soon as we get in the room, a wind hits us and Adam Eget points to the window, where a telephone-size hole explains everything. The couch is covered with candy-bar wrappers and empty ice cream cartons and my bum of a secretary, fast asleep. Beside him is a pill bottle, tipped on its side, with pills spilled everywhere. "Wake up, Keane," I say, loud and right in his ear. "Where's my book?"

Adam Eget and I start ransacking the apartment in search of the book, and lucky for us Keane has a bookcase, so that's where we start. I figure out that he's been busy writing, all right. It turns out he's been doing his secretary work for a lot of guys. And we go through every last one of them. There's a book by a guy named J. D.

Salinger; I think he was a middleweight back in the day. But most I've never heard of. William Faulkner, Lawrence Ferlinghetti, William S. Burroughs. There's one by Victor Hugo. I remember him. He was the bearded one who won *Survivor* the first year. Anyways, the point is, Keane has been busy writing for all these clowns. But we go through every single book, and mine isn't here. Mine isn't here.

I get mad as hell and start yelling in Keane's ear, and finally he's awake and starts in with his "Now, see here," and "I'll have you know," and all the rest of that splendid talk of his.

"You'll be surprised to know that I have other projects, Mr. Macdonald, but I understand your concern. The deadline is imminent, and I promise I will have it done."

"You shoulda just told Hugo to wait his turn. Nobody cares about him anyway. He was from season one, wasn't he?" And I can hear my words getting louder and angrier. But the truth is, I'm scared. "And let's get serious, Keane. Hell, how hard can this be? I mean, don't I phone every few days and tell you lots of stories? All you have to do is type them. Did you get my story about how I had my very own show and that I wanted to call it *The Big Boss Man* and they wanted to call it *The Norm Show*? And how they gave me my very own show but refused to give me a gun? Did you not get that one? I called it in two days ago and must have talked for an hour on your answering machine. That's gotta be good for a chapter or two."

"Yes, I listened to it and, frankly, I didn't understand a word of it."

"Now, you listen to me, old man, it's not your job to frankly understand a word of it. It's your job to type down the words you frankly don't understand and to put them in a book. We gotta hand it in to that Grau broad over at Random House and get our cash."

"Yes, I understand how the process works," and now it's Keane whose voice takes on an angry edge.

We are really starting to shout each other down now, but just when I think it's sure to come to fists, Keane stops, and a faraway look comes upon his eyes and he smiles. "Yes. Yes, now that I think of it, you're quite right, Mr. Macdonald. Why, there's no reason I shouldn't be able to finish this book within that time, what with all the fine material you've been providing me. Certainly, yes. There's just one thing I must insist on. One thing, and I hope it doesn't come off rude. It's just that I mustn't be disturbed, you understand. My work demands solitude. You boys look exhausted. Why don't you get yourself some sleep, and I'll get right to work. Whaddya say, fellows?"

This turnaround by Keane gets me excited, and I lead him over to the desk, where his computer sits. But then when I look over at Adam Eget, I see the tears, so I take the smile off my face. I know the problem, of course, and approach him. "You're thinking about Sammi, aren't you?"

"Yeah, I am," he says. "You know, Norm, I don't know which hurts more—the knowledge that I'll never feel her lips against mine or the knowledge that she was a man who stole my 1.6-million-dollar video-keno ticket."

"For me it would be the second one."

"Really?"

"Oh, yeah, the second one for sure."

"You're a good friend, Norm."

"Better than you think," I say, and pull out a bottle of 150-proof Iceberg rum. "Go into Keane's room, drink down this bottle, and get some shuteye. You need it, buddy." And Adam Eget smiles at the sight of Edward McClintock's bottle and grabs it by the throat like a bad man, and the two of them retire to the bedroom.

I turn my attention back to Keane, who is sitting in front of his computer but not looking at it. Instead, his gaze falls somewhere in the middle distance, where reality resides. "Oh, I don't mean to be inhospitable, but you boys aren't thinking of staying here with me, are you?"

"Sure we are," I say. "Listen. What do you say I sit beside you so we can hurry this up? I'll do the talking and you do the typing, and I bet we'll be finished by the morning."

It looks like my words have snapped Keane out of his trance.

"No need, my good man, no need at all. You could do something to help, though."

"Yeah, sure, Keane, anything at all."

"The thing is, there's been quite a draft here in the parlor ever since the telephone left. I've been helping myself to your clothes. As I explained to you, I'm a method writer. But the thing is, the outfit has gotten a little bit gamey."

"Yeah, yeah, sure." Keane always did take a long time to ask a short question. I grab a *Norm Show* T-shirt, an *SNL* jacket, and a *Dirty Work* cap from my suitcase.

"Mr. Macdonald, I can't help but notice the stitching on your *SNL* jacket."

"Oh, yeah," I say. "The first shipment I bought, the damn fool wrote my name as 'Norm Macfonald.' But he gave them to me half-price and I figured maybe they'd have antique value one day. I got ten like that and never wear them, so you help yourself to one. They're practically brand-new. You'll be wearing a genuine collector's item, Keane."

"Well, thank you very much, Mr. Macfonald."

I guess that's Keane's idea of a joke. "Yeah, no problem at all. There are nine more where that came from. How's that sound?"

Keane smiles. "It sounds splendid," he says, and then flinches.

I just smile at the old man. He's not so bad.

He insists he will have the book finished by the morning but only if I leave him alone. He says I can sleep in his room, and when I look back, Keane is already hard at work, so I hit the hay and fall fast asleep, happy that when I wake up the book will be finished or close to it. But I wake up in the middle of the night when nature calls. I get up and take a visit to the little boys' room, and when I walk out of Keane's bedroom I see something I will likely never forget. There stands Keane fully dressed in my clothes, on top of a small stepladder, with a noose around his neck. He sees me, and I can see the shock register on his face. He's been caught.

Still, he is determined.

"Mr. Macdonald, might I suggest that you go back to your room. This is not something you want to see."

"You're damned right it's not," I say. "But it's not something you want to do either, Keane. Think about it. You slip at all and lose your footing on that stepladder, and you're a dead man."

Things become worse when I look across the room and see Adam Eget in his PJs, looking on in confusion. "You guys woke me up. Hey, what's Mr. Keane doing, Norm?"

I look at him in his pajamas and his innocence. "It's called auto-erotic asphyxiation, Adam Eget."

"No, no. What?" protests Keane.

"What's autoerotic asphyxiation, Norm?"

"Well, it's a very fancy name for a very filthy thing."

"That's not what's going on here," says Keane.

"No, of course not. You were changing a lightbulb, I'm sure. WITH A NOOSE AROUND YOUR NECK."

"Look, I'm warning you two. Just return to your rooms and go to sleep. If you stay, you're not going to like what you see."

"DUH," I say. "Look, if you're hell-bent on doing this thing that only serves to make a filthy thing filthier, then fine. But it is the responsibility of my friend and me to make sure nothing goes wrong. The last thing I want is to try to explain to your friends and family and the press what we witnessed here tonight. Adam Eget, steady the ladder while he deprives himself of oxygen and lays down with himself simultaneously. Something in my book must have filled him with impure thoughts."

"Stop this babble," Keane blares, and removes the noose from his neck. "I've decided against it."

"You're making a wise decision, Keane, and I'll reward you for it." I pull a capsule of amyl nitrite from my pocket. "You go now and lay beside yourself and, at the moment of sin, break this beneath your nose and inhale deeply. It'll do the trick just fine, no rope necessary."

Keane throws the capsule with contempt to the floor, and it bounces once on the hardwood and vanishes beneath the couch.

Immediately, Adam Eget is on his hands and knees with his head underneath the couch, searching for the amyl nitrite as a swine would truffles.

"I suppose you're right, Mr. Macdonald," Keane hisses as I make my way to the little boys' room. "I promised Ms. Grau a manuscript, and I must honor that promise." And, as if in a trance, he trundles over to his computer and sits before it.

I've been biding my time, and now is my chance. I wake up to find Macdonald gone and the other one asleep. Mr. Macdonald has been keeping me captive for a month now. I've been here typing what he says, getting as many words down as possible. The other one has a gun trained on me at all times. They are hiding, they say, from the fat man with the artificial hair. And they might well be. This fat man with the artificial hair may well kill us all. There is a problem, though. He may not exist. I may have made him up. I can't be sure of anything anymore.

In order to fill up Mr. Macdonald's memoirs, I had to stray far from the prosaic facts that made up his life and I have veered into straight-out falsehoods. Why would these fools have barricaded themselves in my brownstone if there was not real danger outside? And what about the dolt sleeping on the couch, the one I named Adam Eget? He never existed before I constructed him on my computer. He does not exist in the real world; he has never managed The World Famous Comedy Store. I know I made him up. But how is it that I could have made up a human being who now lies snoring on my chesterfield? No, this is the truth. I am a secretary, just as Mr. Macdonald has asserted from the beginning. I know that the two live here with me, and they are on the lam. I know this is true and not something I have written. And I know what I need to find Macdonald's essence. I've known it from the start. I tie a band around my biceps, pick up a syrette, place the needle in the crook of my arm, and push hard, just like I've seen Mr. Macdonald do, sending a triple shot of morphine into my blood. It feels just like happiness. I pick up the gun from where it lies beneath the couch and I make for the door. Before I leave, I look in the mirror and am confronted by a slovenly fool. My eyes have gone blank, just like his. I am stunned for a moment. It has finally happened. I have become him. God help me, I have become him.

43

ESCAPE!

strike Adam Eget awake, and he whimpers and asks where he is and who I am and all those questions men ask when they are awoken suddenly.

"Where's Keane? We said we would take turns guarding him, and now he is gone."

"I must have fallen asleep."

I punch him directly in the nose, right in that spot that makes the blood come out fast and full, and Adam Eget covers his nose with his hand and runs crying to the bathroom.

I'm very scared now. Keane wasted too much time, and the thirty-day limit has come and gone. The red Cadillac has been parked across the street for a week now, and some goons knocked on the door a few days ago. Adam Eget and I listened from the closet as Keane answered a few questions and the goons moved on. Since then there's been nothing. But they know we're in the building. I hope Keane remembered that when he left. If he was smart he took the fire escape and then ducked through the kitchen of the Chinese restaurant to Sixth Avenue and beyond. But he's been acting screwy lately, reckless. Sometimes he'll open the curtain in front of the window with the hole in it, sending Adam Eget and me diving behind furniture, because we can still see the big red Cadillac across the street. Does he really think he has a chance against the fat man with the artificial hair?

I reach under the couch for my gun and it's gone. Where the hell did I leave it? I can't go out in New York City unarmed. Keane has a whole bunch of baseball gloves and balls and bats signed by famous players. He's got so many you'd think he was a baseball player himself. I grab the biggest bat I can find, signed by Lou Gehrig. It's not much of a weapon, but it's all I got and I have no time. I have to find Keane and find him fast.

I order a glass of Wild Turkey 101 and ask the waiter to leave the bottle. I have never had much tolerance for libations, but I am determined to go through with this transformation as far as I can. And I see now that the drink has little effect on me. The morphine has numbed me out and the liquor does not burn my gullet. It's like my insides are as impervious as ice. When I talk—and I do feel like talking a lot on this drug—my voice is a slur, thick and incoherent, and I smile and laugh for little reason. It takes only a moment for someone to recognize the voice.

"Hey, I know you." And he is over by me in a moment and has me in a headlock. "You're that guy," he says, leading me to the table where his friends are sitting. "Hey, you know who this guy is?" I can't tell if the question is rhetorical or genuine. One couple there clearly has no idea, but they seem polite enough about it, even a little apologetic. But in the other five I see that their eyes are narrowed in on me, and they look from me to a place down on the table or on the wall, where their memories are just out of reach.

"I seen you in something," offers one.

"Sure you have," I say.

"Where have I seen you?"

Luckily, I have become a bit of an expert on who I am, so I decide to guess from their age how they might know me.

"Well, you may have heard of a little movie called Billy Madison.*"*

"You're not Adam Sandler," one punk sneers dismissively.

"Maybe not, but I know him and he knows me too."

"Then get him on the phone."

"I would, but not for the likes of you."

"Then just tell us how we know you."

"Take it easy, Charley. After all, I invited him over here." This one is the biggest and youngest, and I can tell that he has a dangerous bite to him. But the fine morphine has me immune to my usual fear of the young.

"You ever heard of The Norm Show?*"*

"Nope."

"I played Norm."

"You ever been on television?"

"Are you not even listening? I've been on every talk show there is. Jimmy Fallon, Conan, Kimmel, Leno. Even the grand old man himself, David Letterman. And always as the first guest too." I can feel the pride swelling me up, and I take another fine free shot of booze. This is turning out okay. As long as these fools don't figure out where they almost know me from, they have no choice. Everything is free. So I decide to let the mystery play out. Then I'll let them in on the fine secret, and we'll all have a good laugh and talk about the great merriment I've brought into each of their banal lives.

The one they call Fred says, *"I'm sorry, I never watch TV."* You can tell he isn't sorry at all but proud and probably lying to boot, and I feel my hand turn to a fist under the table. I spend my whole life trying to get on TV, and it just isn't enough for this sonofabitchofaFred.

Then one of the bigger of the rogues gets an impatient look to him, like my life isn't worth the time of a parlor game. *"Look, just tell us where we know you from. We got girls coming over here to meet us soon. We don't have all day."*

"I guess they must have got lost in traffic, huh?" I say, and recognize the line from my audience interaction on those thousands of tapes back at the brownstone. This gets me my first laugh from the table, and it gives me the idea that maybe one of these boys has seen me perform live, in the flesh.

So I give it a thought. Who am I, anyway? I've always felt a man is what a man does, so I give them the truth. *"I've done stand-up com-*

edy across this country, and Canada as well, for nearly thirty years, and I continue to do it to this very day." I have to snort back a laugh, because it sounds like one of those game-show questions where you follow it up with "Who am I?"

"You know Louis C.K.?"

"You know Amy Schumer?"

"You know Aziz Ansari?"

"You know Bill Burr?"

"I know them all, Goddammit, and they know me too!"

I met Louis C.K. once.

"We saw Aziz at Carnegie Hall. You ever play Carnegie Hall?"

"I don't like big rooms. I play clubs. It's more intimate."

"Yeah, I bet you like it real intimate."

I can't tell if this last one is a dig at the size of the venues I play or the more-squalid obvious. Either way, I've already accepted that I am in the company of philistines.

The piling on has brought out the best in one of the fellows, though, and he pushes a brown plastic bowl of bar snacks in my direction. "I was at the Cellar last night and saw Colin Quinn. You know him?"

"Now you're getting closer." I near burst out of my seat and realize that for the first time it is becoming important to me that one of these young men solve this puzzle. "Yeah, me and Colin go way back, and if you know Colin Quinn, there's a good chance you know me too."

And then it happens.

"You're from SNL!"

The chatter gets busy fast. They all know me now, even the one named Fred, who hardly knew what a television was. They pat me hard on the back and laugh and order a pitcher of beer. I demand Wild Turkey 101. They didn't have much choice. I have them over a barrel. If there isn't a bottle of whiskey on my table, and soon, I am likely to take my famous self and walk it right out into the New York streets. So Charley orders whiskey.

Now a new game gets started. "What's your name?"

I have no time for this. I am only interested in knowing what they think of me, so I just point at the stitching on my SNL jacket.

"Oh, of course," says Charley. "It's Norm Macfonald."

"Hey, Macfonald, I knew it was you the whole time. I was a big fan. You did Weekend Update."

"Yeah, you were dry. You did dry comedy. I like dry comedy."

"I always liked you, Macfonald, but everybody I knew thought you sucked. They just didn't get you like I did. You were dry."

"Well, I didn't like him."

Well, isn't that just like Charley, the big one, the bully, to stop the conversation dead with his big, brawly opinion.

"Hey, c'mon, Charley, it was you invited him over. He was just sitting in the corner minding his own business, muttering to himself."

"I remember him. I was in high school and watched the show 'cause of Sandler and Farley. Then he'd come on talking about politics. He'd do some stupid joke, then just stare at the audience with a big dumb smile on his face. He was never funny."

"Well, I liked him," I shout, way, way too loudly, and it seems every eyeball in the room is on me.

"Everything okay over there?" says the bartender.

"Everything is just fine, my good man. I'd be obliged if you could rustle me up a pen and sheet of paper."

"Sure thing." He takes a pen from a jar and turns a paper menu over to the blank side and hands it to me. He smiles warmly at me and extends his hand. I shake it for a while. Probably too long. I'm just not used to this damn morphine. "Say, any chance of getting your autograph, Mr. Macfonald?"

It doesn't matter how cynical I think I am. I'm always delighted to find out that things in this life still have the capacity to surprise me.

I hunch over the hard oak table and write the final chapter.

44

THE FINAL CHAPTER

T here is the way things are and then the way things appear, and it is the way things appear, even when false, that is often the truest. If I am remembered, it will always be by the four years I spent at *Saturday Night Live* and, maybe even more than that, by the events surrounding my departure from that show. As long as *SNL* exists, then so do I.

When people come to see me do stand-up, it is because somewhere in their memory I live on *SNL,* dressed as a young Burt Reynolds, insisting Alex Trebek refer to me as Turd Ferguson. And they come to see me and I am old and fat and I don't mention *SNL* and I do my answering-machine joke and they are happily disappointed. After the show, they stand beside me and take pictures, the way you would with a donkey at the side of a road. They tell me they are big fans and they don't care what their girlfriends say. They understand me even though they know good and well that nobody else does. I'm dry, they say. The next time I come to their town, they don't show up.

It can be difficult to define yourself by something that happened so long ago and is gone forever. It's like a fellow at the end of the bar telling no one in particular about the silver medal he won in high school track, the one he still wears around his neck.

The only thing an old man can tell a young man is that it goes fast, real fast, and if you're not careful it's too late. Of course, the young man will never understand this truth.

But looking back now, I can see that my life since *SNL* has been a full sprint, trying with all my might to outrun the wolves of irrelevancy snapping at my heels. It has all been in vain, of course. They caught and devoured me years ago. But not completely. Lorne would see to that.

My foot would still make a vague imprint; my self would still cast a faint shadow. And years later, I would write a book. And not only write it but be in it as well.

I think a lot of people feel sorry for you if you were on *SNL* and emerged from the show anything less than a superstar. They assume you must be bitter. But it is impossible for me to be bitter.

I've been lucky.

If I had to sum up my whole life, I guess those are the words I would choose, all right.

When I was a boy, I was sure I'd never make it past Moose Creek, Ontario, Canada. But I've been all over this world. Except for Europe, Asia, Australia, Africa, and South America. Oh, and Antarctica. But that's really splitting hairs. I mean, how many people have ever been to Antarctica?

I never expected to be any more than a common laborer, and I would have considered myself lucky to have achieved that. But I was blessed with so much more.

I'm a stand-up comedian and have been for over a quarter of a century. I've performed thousands of hours, from a small club in Ottawa, Ontario, all the way to a small club in Edmonton, Alberta. Sometimes I get big laughs and think I'm the best stand-up in the whole world, and other times I bomb, and I think I'm not even in the top five. Before I was famous I had a whole bunch of jobs where all I needed was boots. People would look right past me, or if they did look at me, it was with a *mean* look. But when I got famous, people would look at me and smile and wonder where they knew me from. If they flat-out recognized me, they'd laugh and dance like they'd won a prize, and I'd just stand there and smile and feel warmth from their love. So the fame made the world, which is a real cold place, a little less cold.

And as for my gambling, it's true I lost it all a few times. But that's because I always took the long shot and it never came in. But I still have some time before I cross that river. And if you're at the table and you're rolling them bones, then there's no money in playing it safe. You have to take all your chips and put them on double six and watch as every eye goes to you and then to those red dice doing their wild dance and freezing time before finding the cruel green felt.

I've been lucky.

45

ME, MYSELF, AND I

I never should have trusted Adam Eget to keep an eye on Keane. Now my secretary is gone and I have to find him and find him fast. I have no idea how long he's been gone or where he is. We were finally starting to get some good work done. I thought we'd found a way to finish the book and pay off my debts, with me telling all my great stories one after another and Keane typing them down. I even let him throw in a few of his own lines from time to time, to make him feel like he could become a writer himself one day. I talked to Julie just yesterday, and she told me that we were only about a thousand words short of a book. At the rate Keane was typing, we would have been finished in a few days. We were so close. But now Keane is gone. And I am lost on the streets of Manhattan, knowing that if one of the goons from the Cadillac finds me, there's precious little this bat will do. I wander the streets for a long time and pass the Regency House, where I once lived and was happy, but it has been destroyed and replaced with a four-story art gallery. Everything above that is sky. I try to locate the thirty-fifth floor and the apartment that was my home. But it's just sky now and I don't have the imagination. I forgot to change these clothes. Everything I wear says exactly who I am. So now I walk down the street with a huge target on my back, looking for the old fool.

I feel a little cold now, so I hasten my step, knowing I'm only a block away from a crackling fireplace and a warming shot of morphine. I'm sure Mr. Macdonald will feel quite generous once I pull the McSorley's menu from the pocket of my SNL jacket. He will be confused when I first present it, but then I will announce it is the end of the book and the start of the money. And the party will begin and the morphine will flow free and I will take just a little too much and they will all think it was a tragic accident. Until they find this note. The future makes me so happy.

At first I think I'm looking at a mirror that's right in the middle of the street. But no. It's just Keane, doing his best impression of me. I walk straight toward him. It is very important I keep him from making a scene.

Oh, God, it's him. I can see he has violence on his tiny mind. In his hand is the Gehrig bat! My most prized possession! The Gehrig bat! The lout has stolen it and now he clearly means to use it to strike me. I don't care much about myself anymore but I'll be damned if he destroys that historic bat with my skull. I fumble in my pocket for the pistol, pull it out, and aim the best I can.

I see the gun and freeze my step. His grip is weak but he aims right at me. I try to speak reason to him but can tell he can't hear. I'm out of time now and can only hope he misses. Once again, luck is my only out. I see the gun shaking, and his eyes close tight. And there is nothing but that peculiar sound of a gunshot. And then I watch as my secretary's borrowed shirt turns red and he falls forward on the hard New York sidewalk. Behind him, I see the fat man with the

artificial hair get into the back of the red Cadillac before it slowly
drives away.

*I open my eyes to see Mr. Macdonald running full speed away, and I
am on the ground and can't get up. My breath is too shallow for me
to shout or even make a small noise so I reach inside my pocket for
the McSorley's menu and my pen and I understand this will be the
last of my writing. But as soon as I have ahold of it my hand fails me
and the crumpled menu takes off running down the street. I smile,
thinking that Mr. Macdonald will have to finish the story of his life
all by himself. Like all of us, I suppose. And then I smell the pizza. I
know it comes from Ricardo's, across the street from my home, but
it has never smelled this powerful or this good before. All I want
in the world is a slice of Ricardo's pizza, the crust well done, with
mushrooms swimming in red sauce, and nothing else. I am filled with
remorse at what I have done. I try to get up again, to follow the scent
of the pizza, but I slip and fall backward and my head hits the hard
pavement. I use my final breaths to take in the mushroom and the red
sauce and the garlic. Life is so good.*

THE LAST PART OF THE WHOLE BOOK

Well this is the last part of the whole book. my secretary went and got himself killed. i got so mad at adam eget cause he was supposed to be guarding him but was sleeping instead so i find a bat and start hitting him with it and he gets down on his hands and knees to protect himself and thats when he finds it. norm, this is your memoir. i found it. i found it. and im happy so i say read it to be sure and adam eget opens it and thats when theres a knock at the door and me and adam eget get quiet and scared cause we know its those goons that work for the fat man with the artificial hair. i take my bat and go to the door and open it and the goon has some sort of costume on and is holding a little piece of paper and singing so i hit him with the bat and he falls in a crumple out cold and i take the piece of paper and it looks like a telegram and the words on it rhyme and its about somebody called terence keane and a book he wrote called the house painter and how some book company wants to buy it but the whole thing rhymes remember so i sing it to adam eget and he tells me that terence keane was the name of my secretary and that my secretary must have called my book the house painter and tried to sell it on the side and then he says look out the window norm look out the window so i look out the window and theres a big blue truck with the words western union on it and it is sitting in the same place that the red cadillac used to sit. hes gone! yes adam eget we got very lucky this day i say and then we run away to the alley and get in the challenger and then we drive away. adam eget says he doesnt want to read the book because reading makes him sleepy and i tell him not to worry nobody needs to read the fucking thing but just to count the words because a book has to be so many words and this one has to be seventy five thousand words and thats how many words a mans life has to add up to but then i think that every man is different and that a nobody like adam egets life probably adds up to a hundred words or something but a bigshot like me my life probably adds up to over a million words or even a billion words so i take the tape recorder and start talking into it fast and adam eget is counting words and i just keep speaking words into the tape recorder because the faster i read the more words go into my book and each word is a part of my life even if the words dont make any sense because they dont have to because thats not in the contract. nobody ever said your life had to make a damn bit of sense just as long as it had enough words thats all. we stop at a bar and adam eget says will you take a look at her ass so i look at the waitresses ass and he says tell me thats not going into the book and i say no its not and he says youre telling me that youre not putting that waitresses ass into the book and i tell him no and he says im crazy if i dont put her ass in the book and i tell him hes so stupid he doesnt even know what should be in a book. i tell him it has to be real important stuff especially in the end part of a book and besides no book in the whole world is supposed to be about a waitresses ass and adam eget starts pouting and says whats so special about you that youre better than a waitresses ass and i say im famous thats what and he says whats that ever got you so i look at the stupid idiot and i say ill show you what its got me ill show you right now and i yell hey waiter get over here cause im hungry and he comes over and i ask him what the special is and im lucky cause its chili and not that stupid fucking turkey chili that i hate either but real chili with pieces of beef in it and so i say hmmmmm to stall for time hmmmm and then my finger starts pointing at my name on my snl jacket and some time passes before the waiter says hey arent you famous and i say sure i am and he says you can have the chili for free and i say i want a whole bowl and not a cup and plenty of crackers too and the waiter agrees to the whole thing. im pretty pleased with myself and i look over at adam eget but he isnt sitting beside me anymore cause he is at the other side of the bar standing in front of a tv so i go over to him and he is talking like a robot and he says the toronto blue jays will win their baseball match tonight by two scores and i cant believe what im hearing so i hit adam eget hard on the side of his head and he falls in a crumple out cold. people come around to see what the trouble is and i tell them im a really famous guy and if they dont believe me they can all just read my clothes and i tell them adam eget is a nobody whose life is worth like a hundred words. everyone is cool with that and it makes me think that thats another thing that fame gets you. you can just go ahead and hit a guy hard on the side of his head. i go back to my table and wait for my food and look around the bar to see where the waitresses ass went and then finally the waiter comes back and he says he is sorry but they are just out of chili but that if i want i can have a bowl of turkey chili. can you believe it. turkey fucking chili. story of my life.

ACKNOWLEDGMENTS

A lot of people need to be thanked, including ones I forget to thank.

All begins with family. Thanks to my brother Leslie, for his outstanding memory of childhood, remembering in detail stories I've long forgotten.

Thanks to my brother Neil, the real writer, whom I read and learn from.

Thanks to my mother, to whom I owe everything. She is beautiful and kind and generous.

Thanks to my father, who is gone but thought of fondly and often. We will meet again, Dad, in the place you live and I cannot imagine.

Thanks to my son, Dylan, who is a good man and a better writer than me, and helped me to write this book.

Thanks to the gals at Spiegel & Grau, headed by Julie Grau. She believed in me and left me be, a fine gift. Laura Van der Veer would talk to me anytime I had a question. Thank you, Laura. And thanks to my agent Joe Veltre, whose instincts were always spot on, for guiding me.

Thanks to Howie Wagman and Mark Breslin, for thinking I could do stand-up before I did. Thanks to the stand-ups: Kinison, Spade, Schneider, and, of course, the Sandman. Without Adam, no career. Thankfully Adam is a generous man with enough ambition for the both of us.

Thanks to Dennis Miller, for giving me my first job and for so much more. Thanks to Roseanne, who taught me to fight. Thanks to Bruce Helford, who taught me to write sixteen hours a day.

Thanks to Lorne Michaels, for fighting for me; to Jim Downey, the best writer ever at *SNL;* to Steve Higgins, for writing sketches with me and convincing me that people would laugh at "Turd Ferguson" and for helping me make a great comedy album, along with the great Brooks Arthur. Thanks to Steve O'Donnell, who is a comedy writer of the very highest order.

Thanks to Lori Jo Hoekstra, for becoming my producing partner. You have to be good at a thousand things in Hollywood. I am good at one and Lori Jo is good at the rest.

Thanks to Marc Gurvitz, who always gave as much time and effort to me as he did his successful clients.

Thanks to David Letterman, who made me laugh for years, who then made my dream come true, and who then, surprisingly, made me his friend.

And, finally, thanks to two of the best writers in the world, for their friendship: Billy Joe Shaver, the first outlaw in country music, who can write the biggest ideas with the smallest of words; and Louis C.K., who was great when I first saw him and is much greater now. These two men I talk to often. Billy Joe is always on the road and loves it. Louis and I talk about how, one day, we will retire to the road, to the greatest thing there is, and to what we do best: stand-up comedy.

ABOUT THE AUTHOR

NORM MACDONALD is a stand-up comedian, writer, and actor who lives in Los Angeles. He is the proud father of Devery.